The Helper

DAVID TURNER

Dedication

To my spiritual father, Harry Gomes...You are the chariot and the horses to my life! I strive to imitate you as you imitate Jesus Christ.

Never have I seen such humility combined with so much power like you demonstrate. You exemplify the heart of the Father...always teaching, uplifting, encouraging, and supporting.

Your unwavering faithfulness and dedication toward our God and His Kingdom are the inspiration that directs my life.

You have influenced and impacted my life like no other.

I give constant praise and thanks to Jesus for loving me so much that he gave me a gift like you!

TABLE OF CONTENTS

INTRODUCTION

Jesus said, "Nevertheless I tell you the truth. It is to your advantage that I go away; for if I do not go away the Helper will not come to you; but if I depart I will send Him to you." (John 16:7) He also said, "I will pray to the Father and He will give you another Helper, that He may abide with you forever." (John 14:16)

Who is this "Helper"? The Holy Spirit. He is our teacher, guide, counselor, comforter, strengthener, and standby. He is the Spirit of Truth, Grace, Mercy and Love. He is the Spirit of Prayer, Intercession, Judgement, and Burning. He is the Spirit of Wisdom, Knowledge, Understanding, Council, Might, and Fear of the Lord. He is also the Spirit of Jesus Christ, Jehovah, Resurrection, Glory, Life, Prophesy, Holiness, and Adoption. He is the Everlasting Spirit, the Good Spirit, and the Standard Spirit...and Oh, yes, He is our Helper!

What is the Holy Spirit here to help us with?

Many people are hoping and praying for Him to help them with finances, a car, a house; maybe to find a spouse. He will do some of these things, as well, when we seek first the Kingdom (Matthew 6:33). The key is to seek His presence and not only His promise (which is provision and protection). However, the main thing the Holy Spirit is here to help us with is to lift up Jesus! (John 16:13-14)

That is why, when we start lifting up the name of Jesus, the Holy Spirit comes! When the Holy Spirit comes, the anointing (of the Holy Spirit) breaks the yoke that is upon the people. (Isaiah 10:27) When the yoke is broken, the people walk in freedom. That is why 2 Corinthians 3:17 says, "Where the Spirit of the Lord is, there is freedom!" He is here to draw us unto Jesus. Unless the Holy Spirit draws a person, they can not come. (John 6:44)

Here is a great secret I have learned...Jesus said, "The Spirit of the Lord is Upon Me to set the prisoners and captives free, to heal the sick, and proclaim the favorable year of the Lord." (Isaiah 61:2/Luke 4:18) The Bible also says, "Greater is He who is in me, than he who is in the world." (1 John 4:4) This means that when the Holy Spirit is upon me, it is for the benefit of others. When the Holy Spirit is in me, it is for my benefit!

Come, ask, see, what God Almighty will do for you, as you are filled with the Good Spirit, The Holy Spirit of God... Your Helper.

CHAPTER ONE

The Good Influence of the Holy Spirit

As believers, it is good for us to be in the world, but not for the world to be in us.

It is good for a boat to be in the water, but not good for water to be in the boat. When a boat is in the water, it moves forward easily. When water is in the boat, it will sink and drown. The Holy Spirit will move us in the direction God has set for our lives when we choose to be influenced by Him.

As the people of God, we must be influenced by the Holy Spirit of Almighty God. Only then, can we influence believers and the world around us.

God has appointed us in order to build His Kingdom. The Apostle Paul describes the meaning of the Kingdom of God. It is not a matter of eating or drinking; but rather of peace, joy and righteousness in the Holy Spirit. (Romans 14:17) As children of God, we are called to build His Kingdom. This means we must lead the people around us towards the peace, joy and righteousness of God. If we ourselves struggle with peace, joy and righteousness in our own lives, how can we impact and expand God's Kingdom?

We fulfill our jobs to lead people to the Kingdom of God when we allow the Holy Spirit to help us. Our Lord Jesus Christ teaches how the Holy Spirit influences us when he shared one of the kingdom principles (Matthew 13:33).

He told of a woman who took a little bit of leaven and hid it in three measures of meal till the whole lump was leavened. The leaven was minute compared to the meal, but the lump grew larger as a result of its presence. When the lump was leavened, three things happened.

It expanded.

It rose up.

It made the dough lighter.

Believers can be compared to the meal or flour, and the Holy Spirit to the leaven. A batch of dough is small until it is leavened. Even though we are small, when we are controlled by the Holy Spirit, God can expand our influence to impact His Kingdom in a big way.

God always wants us to expand and grow. When Jesus Christ sojourned on this earth, we see in Luke 2:52 that He grew in wisdom, stature, grace before God, and favor before men. Is this not wonderful? With the Holy Spirit in us, we can grow in the same way. God's plan is that He wants His Kingdom to expand, and He wants us to work constantly toward that end. (Isaiah 54:2-4) That expansion won't come from the east or west; instead, it comes from God. (Psalm 75:6-7)

We see a man in the Bible named Jabez; his name means "pain and sorrow." This man cried for God to expand his territory (1 Chronicles 4:9-10) The prayer was for God to expand His kingdom through Jabez's life, not for personal gain. God heard his prayer, expanded his territory and named a city after him. (1 Chronicle 2:55)

When you have the leavening effect of the Holy Spirit in your life, God will constantly use you to expand His Kingdom. When leaven is mixed with flour, the dough will rise up. In the same way, God wants each of us to rise up and shine for His Kingdom, for He is our Light. (Isaiah 60:1) When His light dawns in us, we no longer sit and brood in the darkness. We must rise up and shine for His Glory! God wants to cut off all the chains of iron and ropes of sin from around our necks. (Isaiah 52:2-3) He wants us to rise up! Only when we rise up will we be able to move and accomplish His purpose in our lives.

God had a plan and purpose for our forefather Abraham. He received his blessing by his willingness to hear, obey, arise and walk. Abraham lost everything when Lot, his nephew, took all the beautiful property near the Jordan. Then God spoke to Abraham and said, "Arise, look to the north, south, east and west. Walk and tread upon the land, and I will give those places to you and to your descendants." (Genesis 13:14-16) Our God is a generational God. When Abraham arose and walked, not only did it bring about his own blessing, but his descendants, the Israelites inherited the Promise Land. Just like leaven affects the flour, the Holy Spirit can influence your life so that it can be used in the Kingdom of God for now and generations to come.

God's Kingdom principles never work according to human principles As the woman added leaven to the dough, it was made lighter and grew against the laws of nature. Newton's third law tells us that for every action, there is an equal and opposite reaction. For example, if you throw a stone up, it will fall back down. This is the law of gravity; a universally accepted human principle. However, when you are influenced by the Holy Spirit, you can work against the laws of nature to fulfill God's call. The Bible calls these miracles, signs and wonders.

There are several examples in the Bible of God's principles overriding natural law. Jesus Christ was born in the flesh, died on the Cross and rose from the dead on the third day. He was able to enter through a closed door because He was in a spiritual body. Jesus came inside the room where the disciples were gathered and told them not to fear. After coming inside, He ate fish along with the disciples in His resurrected body. Jesus then ascended into Heaven on the 40th day. (1 Timothy 3:16 and Luke 24:49-50) Lifting His hands to the sky, Jesus ascended into Heaven against the principles of nature.

Another example we see in the Bible (Acts 8) is when Phillip was transported in the spirit to another place. God moved Philip in the spirit to reveal the Gospel to a Gentile man and expand the kingdom. When you are influenced by the Holy Spirit, the same spirit that transported Phillip is able to transport you and show you places in the spirit.

I encourage you to let your life be "leavened" so that you can impact the Kingdom of God. Just like leaven affects the whole lump, when you are under the good influence of the Holy Spirit, you will be able to impact God's Kingdom in the same measure.

Precious child of God, if you are thinking, "I am unseen. I don't know anyone, and certainly no one knows me." The leaven is also unseen when it is put in the lump. It even appears to be insignificant. God is speaking to you when He said, "A small one I'll make a thousand. A least one I will make a great nation. I will hasten it in my time." (Isaiah 60:22) My God will make you significant and give you authority. Allow your life to be influenced by the Holy Spirit, and just like the leaven causes the whole lump to rise, God will lift you up.

Consider our forefather Enoch who simply walked with God for 300 years. What was God's testimony about him? He pleased God. If you believe there is a God and you please Him, He will reward you. (Hebrews 11:6 and Genesis 5:22-24)

God is more interested in your attitude than your achievement. He is more interested in the motives behind what you do, than what you accomplish.

You may think people will see you only if you have a major platform, significant wealth or you are successful in the world's eyes, but I tell you, God is calling you. God is calling us to have a leavening impact. Our reward is from Heaven in God's timing. God is a just God. Surely He will reward us. (Hebrews 6:10) Even though the leaven in the dough is unseen, its influence is visible and real. Similarly, the Holy Spirit influence in your life is also visible and real—follow it!

Child of God, if you are not under the good influence of the Holy Spirit, you will be influenced by, your senses, the world and/or the devil.

That is why I encourage you to come under the influence of the Holy Spirit, which is simple:

Decide to live a holy life. God will give you grace. (1 Peter 1:16 / John 1:14-17)

Do not grieve the Holy Spirit. (Ephesians 4:29-31)

Do not quench the Holy Spirit. (1 Thessalonians 5:19)

Here is a simple principle. Do not let bad communication proceed out of your mouth; envy, jealousy, heresy, division, fighting, adultery, clamour, because all of these things hinder the flow of the Holy Spirit. We must ask for the grace of Jesus Christ to get rid of them. He came to baptize us with the Holy Spirit and with fire so we can be overcomers. (Matthew 3:11 / Romans 8:37) When we seek the Holy Spirit's influence in our lives, He will always help us to live holy.

The Apostle Paul emphasizes the need for Holy Spirit in order to come out of backsliding. He writes to the Galatian church, saying, "You did well in the beginning, but now who is entering you, to help you obey the truth" (Galatians 5:7-9). When you face difficult circumstances and situations do not go as you expect, you should not blame God.

You have to understand, your ministry or your walk is not hindered by God. His great love for you desires to remove every obstacle and crooked path created by Satan and make it straight. He wants to go before you and help you in the midst of your difficult situations so you can rise up for His Glory. (Micah 2:13, Isaiah 45:1)

A little leaven leavens the whole lump. If you receive the Holy Spirit in your life, God will take you unto your destiny. God's people often think like politicians, using schemes and techniques to gather people. They choose to walk in the way of the world, instead of the wisdom of God. We must understand one thing: we must be influenced only by the Holy Spirit. If we want to expand, and rise up, we must yield to the Holy Spirit. Only then can we do good work that helps people and exerts influence for the Kingdom of God.

CHAPTER TWO

Beware of Evil Influences

We must learn to discern the difference between the wisdom that comes from God, versus the wisdom that is not from God. If we are not influenced by the Holy Spirit, evil influences are waiting to catch us and cause us to backslide, which displeases God. God is pleased when we live as just people with faith in Him alone. (Hebrews 10:38)

The Bible says in James 3:17, that wisdom from God comes from above, from our Heavenly Father who is known as the Father of Heavenly Lights. He gives perfect gifts. In Him there is no variation. (James 1:17) We must depend on the gift of God's wisdom, which is spirit.

When Moses laid his hand upon Joshua, the Spirit of Wisdom came upon him. The people began to heed the voice of Joshua the same way they obeyed Moses. (Deuteronomy 34:9). As the children of God, the same Spirit of Wisdom from Heaven will come upon us.

We see that the Spirit of Wisdom has seven characteristics, and the number seven is symbolic of perfection.

1. Pure – "Blessed are the pure in heart: for they shall see God" (Matthew 5:8). The Holy Spirit will inspire and show you God's plan and purpose. When our heart is pure, even if we make a hundred mistakes, God will always help us and rectify the situation. When our heart is impure and our motives are wrong, we cannot count on God to help us.

2. Peaceful – Wisdom from God is peaceful and will rule over our heart and life. (Colossians 3:15) His peace will be made perfect in us and will run like a river. (Isaiah 26:3 and 48:18)

3. Gentle – God says the meek shall inherit the earth. (Matthew 5:5)

4. Willing to yield – (John 12:24) We must surrender each day. Unless a grain of wheat dies itself, it can't provide growth of a hundredfold. In the same way, unless you yield to the Holy Spirit influence and wisdom that comes from Heaven, you can't achieve anything. You must overcome by dying to sin, self, pride and fear so that the mark of the wisdom of God will dwell in you.

5. Full of mercy – "Blessed are the merciful: for they shall obtain mercy" (Matthew 5:7). As children of God, we are vessels of mercy. We must show mercy—not doctrines, fighting or division. The mercy of God triumphs over all judgment. (James 2:13)

6. Good fruit – The fruit of the spirit is love, joy, peace, patience, kindness, gentleness, goodness, faithfulness, and self control. (Galatians 5:22) Fruit is the mark of God's blessing, and the Holy Spirit will give much fruit. (John 15:7-8)

7. Without partiality – God is not partial to any one person over another. (Acts 10:34)

This is the Spirit of Wisdom that must influence us.

The wisdom that is not from God will have the three characteristics below:

- Earthly

- Sensual

- Demonic

Earthly Wisdom

An earthly person has no thought of Heaven or Hell. As long as they work, they want to earn money, build a house, eat, drink, sleep and enjoy. This is how they think. The god of this age, Satan has blinded the eyes of earthly people regarding eternal values, and they trust in the flesh alone. (2 Corinthians 4:4) Even when good things happen around them, they don't recognize it. (Jeremiah 17:5-6)

An earthly person judges everything. But Jesus Christ said, "Judge not, or you shall be judged." An earthly person can't understand that it is the Holy Spirit alone that convicts people about judgment. (John 16:7-8) An earthly person will one day pay the price, for the wages of sin is death. (Romans 6:23)

As children of God, we must avoid sensual or earthly influences. Christians often fail to realize they are becoming earthly and imitating the world, but earthly influences are now being brought into the church; the vulgarity of the world is rampant. Many are imitating the earthly and sensual mannerisms of the world in their walk, talk and dress, which is why they are not bringing any Holy Spirit influence into the lives of people around them.

Sensual Wisdom

Sensual people are gluttonous, lazy, licentious, often prone to addiction, and believe only what they see. That is why many say miracles stopped with the apostolic times. We must not forget that God is not a physical person; He is Spirit. (John 4:24 and 2 Corinthians 3:17) When we question God, He might not answer immediately. Sensual people want answers immediately. They want to know who God is and how He looks (through their senses.) They will ask, "Where is God? Show me God." They believe truth is only what they feel. "I'm not feeling good about this man/circumstance/etc." Statements like these reveal a sensual outlook and no Holy Spirit influence. Sensual people always think they are different from everyone else. Sensual people can't hear the voice of God because they haven't met God. That is why they say, "When I see, I will believe." Sensual people can't come under the influence of the Holy Spirit because they are too consumed with talking about how they feel. After some years, the sensual person will become an earthly person.

Demonic Influences

If you are not under the influence of the Holy Spirit, the third influence of evil may overtake you—the demonic influence. We see in Mark 5:1-20 a man influenced by the demonic, walking among the tombs. A legion of demons possessed him. (A legion at this time in history was defined as six thousand; this passage indicates this man was possessed by six thousand demons.) When the man saw Jesus, he said, "Son of man, what do you have to do with us?" So demonic or devilish people are constantly under the influence of demonic spirits. They don't possess any meaning of life and they advocate wrong spirits.

Let's take, for example, the practice of yoga in America. People who participate in yoga don't realize how it is influencing them. The poses are imitations of animals and serpents. When people performing yoga are "clearing" the mind and using repetitive chants, they are allowing other spirits—demonic spirits—to enter their minds.

The Holy Spirit never requires us to empty our minds. In fact, we are specifically commanded to fill our minds with thoughts that are lovely, pure, noble and true. (Philippians 4:8) The moment the mind is empty, evil spirits will enter. Failing to walk under the influence of the Holy Spirit is an open invitation to be possessed by other spirits.

When people are exposed to sensual, earthly or demonic influences, the "wisdom" they are receiving is of the devil. We must remember this: Jesus Christ came to destroy the works of Satan. (1 John 3:8) God is calling you to be a spiritual person. When you are under the influence of the Holy Spirit, you will be filled with the fruit of the Spirit and be a spiritual person. (Galatians 5:22)

Worldly wisdom is envious, self seeking and confusing. It will cause those who feed off the world's knowledge to become sensual, earthly or devilish (full of demonic influence). When people choose to pursue the world's way of living, they will not inherit the Kingdom of God. This means they will live under the bondage of confusion, temptation and never be satisfied in fulfilling the good work God has set before them.

However, those who choose to be influenced by the Holy Spirit will walk in the spirit and inherit everything God ordained for their lives. This inheritance comes from being adopted in the Kingdom of God, in which we are called sons and daughters of God. Romans 8:14 says we are able to call God "Abba Father". Everything in the heavenlies becomes ours because we are heirs of God and co-heirs with Jesus Christ.

Choosing to live according to the world will cost us everything we will have in the heavenlies. We will become susceptible to live under bondage, deception and demonic influences. We must choose in this life to be influenced by the Holy Spirit so we may take hold of every good gift God has in store for us.

The Bible says (Joshua 24:14-15) "choose this day whom you will serve. As for me and my house, we will serve the Lord."

We have the option to choose whether to be sensual, earthly and demonic or spiritual people instead. If we go by our own selfish desires, we will be tempted, entangled and drawn away from the goals and heart of God (James 1:14)

Many times when evil influences control our lives, we find ourselves to be tempted, entangled and drawn away. In Genesis chapter 3, we see how evil attracted Eve towards the forbidden fruit when God said not to eat it. Not only did she eat it, but she also gave it to her husband.

That is why our Lord Jesus Christ said, "Spirit knows the spirit; flesh knows the flesh." (Galatians 5:16-20) There are many books and resources people seek to find wisdom, yet only one possesses life and spirit within it's text - the Holy Bible. John 6:63 says, "the words of Jesus Christ are life and spirit. We can receive Biblical wisdom only when the Holy Spirit is in us. The Holy Spirit is the power of God, and the wisdom of God. When the Holy Spirit dwells in us, we will we be continuously under His wisdom in our lives. (1 Corinthians 24:30-31) Jesus Christ came as an ordinary man born in the flesh. (1 Timothy 3:16) He brought heavenly wisdom through the Holy Spirit to influence the earth.

When we have faith in Jesus Christ, we will be known as children of God. (John 1:12) If we are spiritual people, we will desire to simply obey the commandments of the Word of God without questioning or answering back. We see in Joshua 11:15 that what God commanded Moses, Moses obeyed. What Moses commanded Joshua, Joshua obeyed. Obedience brings the blessing. We tend to want everyone to listen and obey to what we say, but we resist obeying God Almighty.

Precious people of God, if we want to be spiritual people, we must obey. Again, if we are not under the influence of the Holy Spirit, we will be influenced by sensual, earthly and demonic forces and will find ourselves tempted, entangled and far away from God.

When people follow their own methods, they often fall into sensual, earthly and demonic traps. Seek always to be a spiritual person under the influence of the Holy Spirit. Many focus on divisions and denominations, instead of sound doctrine and Scriptures inspired by the Holy Spirit. But when our wisdom comes from the Heavenly Father, we will not fall under the influence of sensual, earthly or demonic wisdom.

Jesus Christ was available to everyone, all the time. As a servant of God, are you available? A spiritual, anointed person will be in high demand.

I encourage you to come under the influence of the Holy Spirit wisdom so that God Almighty can bless you in all things.

CHAPTER THREE

Search the Deeper Things of God

You need not discover anything about your life, instead you must uncover what God has already said about you. The Holy Spirit alone can reveal to you the deeper knowledge of God's plans, preparation and purpose in your life. 1 Corinthians 2:9-10 tells us, "no eye has seen, no ear has heard, and no heart can perceive what God has prepared for those who love God." When you are under the influence of the Holy Spirit, He will show you what God has prepared for you.

This is in contrast to when we walk in the way of the world, and therefore we cannot see what God has stored for us. The Bible says, make the heart of this people dull and their ears heavy, and shut their eyes; lest they see with their eyes, hear with their ears and understand with their heart and return to be healed. (Isaiah 6:10 / Matthew 13:14-15)

God's desire is for us to be filled with the Holy Spirit so we can grow deeper in the knowledge of Him. Precious child of God, wherever you are in your relationship with God, he doesn't want to leave you there. If you know Him, like a person dipping their toe in the water, He wants to take you ankle deep. If you know Him to the ankle, He wants to take you to the level of your knees; then to your waist, to your shoulders, and eventually He wants you to swim in the knowledge of God.

We see this when God spoke to the prophet Ezekiel in the temple, the water became like a river that was deeper than a man could stand in—deep enough to swim (Ezekiel 47). The Bible recounts the river of water flowing from the temple to the ocean. The sweet waters of the river revived the dead creatures within the salty, bitter waters of the ocean. Everywhere the river flowed, life was restored. (Ezekiel 47:9)

Child of God, your body is the temple. The living waters is the Holy Spirit that will flow through you. (Hebrews 3:6, John 7:37-38, 1 Corinthians 3:16 and 1 Corinthians 6:19) The Spirit of Truth will flow through you like the living waters to bring the bitter and the backslidden back, which will bring glory to God. The deeper knowledge of God will bring action and fulfillment to God's plans and purpose through your life. When this happens, a man will not boast about himself ("I did this, and I achieved that.") He will give every credit to God Almighty alone.

The mark of the Holy Spirit's influence in your life is walking in truth and glorifying the Lord Jesus Christ. Jesus tells us that when the Spirit of Truth comes, He will lead us into all truth and glorify God. (John 16:13-14)

In addition, when God's Holy Spirit takes you unto deeper experiences, He will help you to know and follow the teachings of Jesus Christ. What the Holy Spirit hears from our Heavenly Father, He will declare it to you; He won't speak on His own.

God Jehovah, Jesus Christ, and the Holy Spirit are one in the Heavens. Everything they do is done in unity. Jesus said, (John 14:10, 14, 24) "The words I speak to you, I do not speak on my own authority, but the Father who dwells in me does the works. If you ask anything in my name, I will do it, so that the Father will be glorified and your joy will be full."

To come in the name of Jesus mean to speak the words Jesus spoke. Then you will have what you ask, the Father will be glorified and your joy will be full.

Jesus Christ foretold that the Holy Spirit, whom the Father would send in His name, would teach all things and bring to our remembrance all things that He said to us. (John 14:26) You must remember that God Almighty, our Heavenly Father, is the God of all comfort. (2 Corinthians 1:4) Jesus Christ comforts us like a mother comforts a child. (Isaiah 66:13) The Father and Son in Heaven have given us the Holy Spirit as a Comforter to put into our remembrance what Jesus Christ spoke. In this instance, comfort comes from confidence in the source of the wisdom. Not only does the Holy Spirit bring the words of Jesus to our rememberance, but gives us the assurance that the word is true and never fails. (2 Corinthians 1:20/ 1 Kings 8:56)

When we are under the unction and influence of the Holy Spirit, we will know all things. But even a prophet will not know things if not under the unction of the Holy Spirit. (1 John 2:20) Unction will make all things known. Under the unction of the Holy Spirit, God showed his ways to Moses. (Psalm 103:7) God also made His acts known to the children of Israel. The same God will help us.

Elisha the prophet was a great prophet. He received a double anointing of the gifts of the Holy Spirit. (2 Kings 2:9-10) However, when he came to the Shunammite woman, her son was dead, but she did not tell the servant of God until he came to her house. Elisha said, "Why has God hidden this from me?" (2 Kings 4) Only when we are under the good influence of the Holy Spirit are we able to know God's plans and purposes, His ways, and His acts in our lives. Holy Spirit influence alone can take you to that deeper knowledge. Jesus said, "No one needs to teach you; the Spirit of Truth will come and lead you in all truth. He will teach you. There is no lie in Him." (I John 2:27)

When we walk in the deeper knowledge of God, there will be transformation in many areas of your life. The

Holy Spirit teaching will help you to do fivefold ministry. You will go from glory to glory. You may start out as a witness, then an evangelist, then God may call you as a teacher, pastor, prophet, and an apostle. All things will happen under the influence of the Holy Spirit. (1 Corinthians 12:28 and Ephesians 4:11-12)

When you understand the love of God upon your life, you will automatically come under the good influence of the Holy Spirit. God loved the world so much that He gave His Son Jesus that whosoever believes in Him shall not perish, but have everlasting life. (John 3:16) God loved you and me so much. He is the God of Love. (1 John 4:8) That love is not an ordinary love.

In your life, when you have the deep knowledge of God and you are under the influence of the Holy Spirit, you will always acknowledge the grace of Jesus Christ. We are not saved by works, but by grace (through faith in Jesus Christ). (Ephesians 2:8)

In the same way, when you are under the good influence of the Holy Spirit and have a deeper knowledge of God, you never lose your communion with the Holy Spirit and will always want to have communion with Him. (2 Corinthians 13:14—love of Father God, grace of Lord Jesus Christ, fellowship and unity of the Holy Spirit) May God Almighty give you the same communion.

May you have a deeper knowledge of God's plans and purpose in your life. (1 Corinthians 2:10) Let the Holy Spirit of God search the deep things of God in your life.

What no eye has seen, no ear has heard, and no heart has perceived God has prepared for you because you love Him.

CHAPTER FOUR

The Spirit of Wisdom

When influenced by the Holy Spirit, what we do will be pleasing to God. (Psalm 143:10) King David said, "God, teach me to do Your will. Lead me unto the land of the plain by Your good spirit." Teach me to do your will in the original Hebrew means, Teach me the way in which I am able to please You, God. So when we are under the influence of the good Spirit, our thought process becomes, "How can I please Almighty God?"

We previously discussed how people can be under the influence of sensual, earthly or demonic influences. If we don't have the Holy Spirit, we will fall under one of these categories. (James 3:15) But when we are under the influence of the Holy Spirit, life will be entirely different.

When Moses laid his hands on Joshua, the Spirit of Wisdom came upon him. Just as the people heeded the voice of Moses, they began to heed the voice of Joshua in the same way. (Deuteronomy 34:9-10) That Spirit of Wisdom comes to us through the Holy Spirit, and we must seek it so that our lives will be blessed. In turn, we will be a blessing to others. Ephesians 1:17 declares, "That the God of our Lord Jesus Christ, the Father of glory, may give unto you the Spirit of Wisdom and revelation in the knowledge of him."

The revelation of the knowledge of God comes only when we are under the influence of the Spirit of Wisdom. God alone can give us this, and it is given when we pray for it. The Holy Spirit will influence our level of wisdom, for He is the Spirit of Wisdom. Before the Lord Jesus Christ was born, Isaiah the prophet spoke about the seven spirits upon the Lord Jesus Christ, who is the Root of Jesse, and mentioned the Spirit of Wisdom. (Isaiah 11:2)

Wisdom is the ability to apply the knowledge, experience, common sense, insight and understanding that we have. That is why God encourages us to seek wisdom in whatever area we lack it.When we ask the Heavenly Father, Who is the Father of Heavenly Lights, He will give us good and perfect gifts. He is more than pleased to give us the Spirit of Wisdom as a gift in our lives. (James 1:5, 6 and 17 and 2 Corinthians 12:8-10) As we seek to obtain the Spirit of Wisdom, be influenced by it, and apply it, we must begin with the fear of God...for the fear of God is the beginning of wisdom. (Proverbs 9:10, Job 28:28)

In Genesis 37:1-11, we read about Joseph, the eleventh son of Jacob. Joseph received visions from God and declared those visions to his brothers and father. In one vision, he saw the wheat chaff bowing down to him. In another vision, the sun, moon and stars were all bowing down and worshipping Joseph. When he told his family what he had seen, they all became angry and accused him of being a dreamer. But Jacob kept in his heart the visions Joseph shared. Just as He did to Joseph, our Heavenly Father will impart supernatural wisdom to our lives through visions and dreams.

Out of greed and jealousy, Joseph's brothers threw him in a pit and sold him. He ended up in Potiphar's house as a slave, but he became a successful man because God was with him. In fact, he became the boss of the house. Potiphar saw that God was with Joseph and whatever he did was prosperous. For Joseph's sake, God started blessing the house of Potiphar. (Genesis 39:2-5)

It's important to remember that when God is promoting and helping us, the devil will also try to attract us with the works of the flesh which are defined very clearly as adultery, fornication, uncleanliness, lasciviousness, idolatry, sorcery, hatred, contention, jealousy, outbursts of wrath, selfish ambition, dissensions, heresies, envy, murder, drunkenness and revelings. (Galatians 5:19-21) Potiphar's wife tried to entice Joseph to fall into a trap and have sexual relations with her, but Joseph refused to commit such a wicked act because he feared God and respected his master. He ran away from Potiphar's wife and retained his purity and holiness. (Genesis 39:9)

However, because of the accusations of Potiphar's wife, Joseph was put in prison. Then God gave Joseph favor with the prison officer, and all the prisoners were under his supervision and control. (Genesis 39:20-21) In God's time, God's wisdom made Joseph to stand before Pharaoh and give the interpretation of Pharaoh's dream; and Pharaoh appointed him Prime Minister over the entire land. He became like a father to Pharaoh, a ruler of his household. Pharaoh felt that no one in the entire land had the Spirit of God and was full of wisdom and discernment like Joseph. (Genesis 41:38-41 and Genesis 45:7-9) The same God that promoted Joseph will give us the Spirit of Wisdom today.

Wisdom comes from Heaven. (James 3:17) Don't fall into the trap of thinking that degrees or earthly qualifications will make people wise. We become wise only by accessing God's wisdom. When we possess it, God will bless us. That is why when God gives us wisdom and when we are under the Spirit of Wisdom, that wisdom is supreme. (Proverbs 4:7)

Wisdom is pure, so to have wisdom, we must live a holy, godly life. (1 Peter 1:16) Holy living enables us to see God's plans and purposes in our lives and in the lives of others. Remember that Matthew 5:8 says, "Blessed are the pure in heart: for they shall see God." This verse is referring to seeing God's plans and purposes—not literally seeing God. We know this because the Bible says in John 1:18, "No man has seen God at any time."

Coming back to the example of Joshua, when he received the Spirit of Wisdom, not only did all of the people start heeding the voice of Joshua, but even the sun and the moon stopped when he commanded them at Gibeon and in the valley of Ajalon. (Joshua 10:12-13) God has not heeded the voice of a man in this way either before or since. If we want the power of God on our lives, we must be able to get this kind of wisdom from God.

Moses received God's wisdom when he was in Egypt. Everyone thought he was wise due to what the Egyptians had taught him. (Acts 7:22) But when he received divine wisdom, God spoke to him in a vision and showed the pattern for building the tabernacle of God. In those days, there were no computers, laptops or memory cards. God showed Moses the vision and gave him the wisdom. God made His ways known to Moses. (Psalm 103:7)

To know the plans of God requires divine wisdom. That is what Moses was able to grasp. God said in Exodus 25:8-9, "And let them make me a sanctuary; that I may dwell among them. According to all that I show you, after the pattern of the tabernacle, and the pattern of all the instruments, even so shall you make it." Moses had to get the vision and translate it in order to build the beautiful tabernacle for God.

When Moses laid his hands on Bezaleel, he transferred the good influence of the Spirit of Wisdom. This man who was an architect was able to understand everything. He was able to prepare everything God showed forth in the vision to Moses. This is the power we can have when we are under the Spirit of Wisdom of God. Bezaleel was an artisan. He knew how to craft and work, but divine wisdom made the difference so that he could do exactly what God wanted. He was able to create and prepare every article without even a small mistake. (Exodus 36:1)

Similarly, when we follow Almighty God, our thoughts must always be to please Him. When we have that kind of wisdom, we will not stumble. Ecclesiastes 7:19 is clear that wisdom makes one wise. When we receive this kind of Spirit of Wisdom under the influence of the Holy Spirit, we are more powerful than ten mighty men. What a wonderful blessing!

Ecclesiastes 9:13-18 tells of one small village with a few people in it. A great king came against it and put a bulwark around it. The Bible tells us that one poor wise man was able to deliver that little city from this great king by his wisdom. Even though you may be a small man, the devil wants to bring a big problem upon you. Even though you are going your own way, the devil wants to cast his aspirations upon you. You may be humbly going about your business, but the devil wants to project that you are a prideful man. The devil always wants to attack you in a big way.

Countering and overcoming the enemy and becoming a blessing can be done only with the help of the Spirit of Wisdom. So let us become wise people by obtaining the Spirit of Wisdom from the Heavenly Father like this poor wise man. Let us be able to deliver this generation from sin, sickness, sorrow and problems. Let us lead people towards Jesus Christ Who can deliver them.

To whom is God promising this kind of wisdom?

Ecclesiastes 2:26 explains that when we please God Almighty, He gives us this kind of wisdom; and it enables us to walk with God, talk with God, please God and understand our purpose. We will become prophets in the sight of the Lord. We may be in the midst of issues with our family or our generation, but we will still shine because we have this kind of wisdom.

In Genesis 5:22-24 and Hebrews 11:5-6, we read about Enoch who walked with God for 300 years. What is his testimony before he was physically taken from earth? He pleased God. Without putting our faith in Jesus Christ who is our wisdom (1 Corinthians 1:24), it is impossible to please our Heavenly Father. When we please our Heavenly Father, when we trust Him, He will give us a great reward. When Joseph got that kind of wisdom from God, the king rewarded him. He put gold chains and precious garments upon him. Joseph was made a ruler. God will give the same kind of blessing in our lives.

Though Daniel was carried as a slave to Babylon, he was able to tell the king what he had dreamed and the interpretation of the dream. (Daniel 2:21 and 2 Timothy 3:15) If we seek the Scriptures, God will give us great wisdom for His glory. Luke 21:15 tells us that Jesus Christ gives us words of wisdom which our adversaries are not able to resist. God might open a big and effectual door of ministry, but the adversary always wants to work against it. (1 Corinthians 16:9) You might have a good job, but the people around you might mock you or give you a difficult time. God may have given you a good business, but the competition might try to rise up, slander and pull you down. You may be called into ministry, but some people don't want to let you grow due to jealousy. How are we able to overcome? When Jesus Christ spoke, no adversary was able to stand against Him. God will impart this same kind of grace to your life. Receive that kind of wisdom.

God gave King Solomon such great wisdom , but because he married foreign women and committed adultery, he wrote in Proverbs 6:32 that the one who commits adultery lacks understanding. (I Kings 4:31) One who joins his spirit with the Lord becomes one spirit with the Lord. (1 Corinthians 6:17) But he who joins his body with an adulterous woman becomes adulterous. We must be careful to obtain pure wisdom from Heaven, then to live pure and under the influence of the Holy Spirit, under the influence of the Spirit of Wisdom in our life. Then no one will be able to stand against us.

Just as God made Daniel, who was a slave, into a great man (Daniel 1:20), we see the same happen to Stephen in the New Testament. He was supervising the food and the needs of the people, and God gave him such great wisdom. (Act 6:10) When we come under the influence of the Holy Spirit and get the Spirit of Wisdom like so many characters in the Bible did, then our life will be a blessing to others.

A Spirit of Wisdom means knowledge guided by understanding. When you obtain the Spirit of Wisdom from the Holy Spirit, whatever knowledge you have is guided by understanding with the help of the Spirit of Wisdom in your life. (Isaiah 11:2 and Exodus 31:3) When that wisdom came upon Jesus Christ, no one was able to speak against Him. We see in Luke 2:52 that Jesus Christ grew in wisdom and stature, with grace before God and favor before men. Our Lord Jesus Christ will always guide us and give us the wisdom we seek. (1 Corinthians 1:24 and Exodus 36:1-2)

In the Old Testament, when people followed God's law, they received this Spirit of Wisdom.(Deuteronomy 4:6) In New Testament times, those who follow Jesus Christ are sanctified and given this kind of wisdom. (1 Corinthians 1:24-30) So when you are washed by the blood of Jesus and have faith in Jesus Christ (Romans 5:1:7-8), you are not becoming righteous; you are already made righteous, and you must maintain that righteousness. In Matthew 5:6, God said, "Blessed are those who hunger and thirst for righteousness: they shall be filled." What will you be filled with when you hunger and thirst for that righteousness? God will fill you with the Spirit of Wisdom. (Proverbs 10:31)

To whom is this kind of wisdom ascribed in the Bible?

We already mentioned Bezalel, who built God's tabernacle according to the vision God gave to Moses. We also see Joseph in Acts 7:9-10, Moses in Acts 7:22, Solomon in 1 Kings 3:12, Stephen in Acts 6:3 and 10, and Paul in 2 Peter 3:15.

These are all people who obtained the Spirit of Wisdom and they were constantly under the influence. God gave these ordinary people supernatural wisdom. Let us all be influenced by that wisdom.

Paul was a murderer, and God made him a great apostle. Stephen was a man looking after the food, but God made him a mighty worker of miracles and an evangelist. Daniel was a slave. Solomon was a king. Moses was a murderer who became a great leader. They are all unique characters in the Bible. In the same way, God will make you a unique personality when you are always seeking the Holy Spirit and the Spirit of Wisdom. He will bless you and take you to a higher level.

What is the value of the wisdom of God? Why do we require that kind of wisdom? Why should we seek His Heavenly wisdom in our life?

People are not content. People grumble. These days most people are not joyful. They are not able to open their hearts and laugh wholeheartedly. When you have godly wisdom, it brings happiness to your life. (Proverbs 3:13)

This Spirit of Wisdom from above has many benefits. It will keep us away from evil and wickedness. (Proverbs 5:1-6) This wisdom is better than rubies. (Proverbs 8:11) It is more precious than gold. (Proverbs 16:16) For these reasons and more, we must determine in our minds today, "God, let me be under the good influence of the

Spirit of Wisdom so that my life will be a blessing." May God put determination in our hearts to seek the Spirit of Wisdom. (Proverbs 23:23)

As believers in the body of Christ, when we earnestly seek Jesus Christ, He will give us this wisdom. (Luke 21:15) God Almighty by His grace can give us that gift today. (1 Corinthians 12:8) We will always be influenced by the Holy Spirit. (Colossians 1:9) When we get this type of wisdom from heaven, it will become a means of instruction in our lives. (Colossians 1:28) Let us all be influenced by the good Spirit, the Spirit of Wisdom from Almighty God.

CHAPTER FIVE

Spirit of Grace

Jesus Christ came to this earth to baptize us with the Holy Spirit and fire just as he received the Holy Spirit, which descended upon him in the form of a dove. At the same time, the voice of the Father spoke from the Heavens, "This is my beloved Son, in whom I am well pleased." (Matthew 3:16-17)

Herein lies the theme: When we are under the influence of the Holy Spirit, we can do all things through Christ who strengthens us. (Philippians 4:13) The Holy Spirit provides strength to our inward man.

How can we get that strength? Only by the Spirit of Grace, the unmerited favor of God.

The Bible says, "Be strong in the grace that is in Christ Jesus." (2 Timothy 2:1) Jesus is the Spirit of Grace. (Zechariah 12:10; Hebrews 10:29) We must let our inward man, our human spirit, be influenced by the Holy Spirit so that we will become one spirit with the Lord. (1 Corinthians 6:17) Then, God is willing to do more for us than we can think or ask. (Ephesians 3:16-20)

Believe that when God asks us to do something, He is able to provide the strength that we need to do it. The key is that His strength comes when we are under the good influence of the Holy Spirit, who enables us to think creatively. Our productivity will increase, and our accomplishments will multiply. We must join our spirit with the Holy Spirit and allow our outward man of negative emotions to perish and our inward man to be renewed day by day. (2 Corinthians 4:16) Then we will delight in the law of God in the inward man. (Romans 7:22)

Allow the Holy Spirit to hover over your human spirit. When the Spirit of God moved and God said, "Let there be light," there was light. (Genesis 1:2-3) Similarly, when the Spirit of God is in control of your human spirit, strength will be created in your inner parts. More than you think or ask will be done.

Why does God want to strengthen the inward man and give us more than we think or ask?

The secret is found in this passage. He wants the Father's name to be glorified through your life. That is why the Bible says in Daniel 11:32, "The people that know their God shall be strong, and do great exploits." May God Almighty give us this kind of strength in our inward man. May we be influenced by the good spirit of Almighty God and do amazing things as a result.

Consider our forefathers and role models, Abraham, Isaac and Jacob; their herds were multiplied. Why? Even when they were in the wilderness, they were under the influence of the Holy Spirit. God always did more than they thought or asked because of His covenant. (Psalm 105:8-9; 1 Chronicles 16:15-20) That is why Paul said, "I have planted, Apollos watered; but God gave the increase." (1 Corinthians 3:6)

Everything is possible under the good influence of the Holy Spirit through Christ (the Anointed One) who dwells in us. The Holy Spirit influences our accomplishments more than we think or ask because we are strengthened by the Holy Spirit. Jesus said, "Without me you can do nothing...If you abide in me, and my words abide in you, you shall ask what you want, and it shall be done for you. You will bear much fruit and my Father will be glorified" (John 15:5, 7-8).

The Bible gives us many examples of how the Holy Spirit influenced different people to accomplish great things for God's glory. Over and over again, we see men used by God to deliver His people from their enemies.

The children of Israel cried to God in Judges 3:9-10, and God raised up a deliverer. His name was Othniel the son of Kenaz, Caleb's younger brother. The Spirit of the Lord came upon Othniel, who went to war against the king of Mesopotamia and won a great victory. When the good influence of the Holy Spirit influences your inner man, the same God will do for you more than you think or ask.

When your inner man is strengthened under the influence of the Holy Spirit, you will be able to gather many people together for a good cause in order to glorify the name of God. You will be able to fight battles and get the victory on God's behalf.

Gideon is another example of God raising up a man to deliver His people. In Judges chapter 6, the Spirit of the Lord came upon Gideon and all the people gathered around him. Gideon expressed to God his fear of the Midianites and reminded God that he was from a small family. He never acknowledged that he was strong enough to do what God asked of him even though God had told him he was strong. God Almighty tells us to get strength by allowing our inward man to be influenced by the Holy Spirit. God said to Gideon in Judges 6:16, "Surely I will be with you, and you shall smite the Midianites as one man."

When the Spirit of the Lord came upon Gideon, he won the battle with only a few men. Without fighting, God created confusion in the camp of the enemy and destroyed them altogether. The Holy Spirit influence in our lives will strengthen us so that we become great leaders and influencers among people. When God touches your human spirit, you will have supernatural strength to achieve great accomplishments for God.

In Judges 14, we read the account of a man named Samson. According to the instructions of God, he went to get married to a Philistine woman in order to take vengeance upon the Philistines. When Samson was on the way to meet with his bride, he came upon a roaring lion. He destroyed and killed the lion as if it had been a young goat. (Judges 14:6)

When the Spirit of the Lord came upon Samson, he received supernatural strength and killed a thousand men at one time. In another instance, his enemies bound him with rope. The ropes that were around his body were loosed by Holy Ghost fire; when the Spirit came, all of the ropes were burnt away. (Judges 14:6; Judges 15:14) That same God will help us today.

When our inward man is influenced and strengthened by the Holy Spirit, the fear of confrontation with our enemies will depart from our lives. (2 Chronicle 24:20) When we are strengthened in our inward man, we will become builders of the house of God. Zechariah 4:6 says, "Not by might, nor by power, but by my spirit, says the Lord of Hosts." This is how we must think. Our personality will be transformed when there is a change in our inward man. We will become brand new people.

In another account, David was an ordinary shepherd boy when he received the anointing of the Holy Spirit. (1 Samuel 16:3) God showed Samuel to go to the house of Jesse and anoint David with oil. From that day onward, the Spirit of the Lord was strong upon him.

What was that anointing that transformed an ordinary shepherd boy into a king?

The Bible says, (Song of Songs 1:2) "that Jesus Christ is the anointed oil poured forth." Symbolically, when Samuel poured oil on David, he was anointing him with Jesus Christ, who is the Spirit of Grace. That Spirit of Grace gave him the wisdom, strength, and discerning to become king.

May we receive the Holy Ghost influence in our inner man so that God can do for us more than we ask or think.When the power of the Holy Spirit power comes, an ordinary man will become supernatural. God who anointed Othniel, Gideon, Sampson, and David, is the same God who will anoint us with the Spirit of Grace today.

CHAPTER SIX

God's Call and Destiny for Your Life

"Your destiny should determine your direction, your direction

should not determine your destiny"

God is calling you. Everyone who is called by His name is created for His glory, to be His witness. He formed you to declare His praise. (Isaiah 43:7, 10, 21) When you obey the call of God and follow the destiny on your life, you will receive a blessing.

But how do we follow the call?

By the Holy Spirit's influence. When we are under the Holy Spirit's influence, we can hear where the Spirit is telling us to go. (Revelation 22:17) We begin to understand

and pursue the call of God on our lives and become a blessing for others when we fulfill His destiny in our lives. God has predestined that call. (2 Corinthians 5:17) He planned to make us like Him. (Romans 8:29) When God predestined our lives, He called us to become the first fruits of Jesus Christ. (1 Corinthians 1:9) God has planned a great destiny for our future. When we reject the call, we reject the special treatment and privilege that God Almighty has prepared for us.

When God predestined, God called. When God called, God justified. When God justified, God glorified. (2 Thessalonians 2:14, Hebrews 9:15) God called us from darkness to marvelous light. (1 Peter 2:9, 3:9) He called us to be a blessing. Hear the call of God and respond.

The Holy Spirit helps us obey God's call. God said, "I will give you a new heart. I will put a new spirit in you. I will cause you to walk in God's statutes and to be careful to observe the ordinances of God." (Ezekiel 36:26-27) This means God can make everything brand new within us so that we will be able to obey His call. God Almighty knew about us before He called us. (Ephesians 1:4/ Jeremiah 1:5-6) The elect are called according to the foreknowledge of the Heavenly Father. (1 Peter 1:2) But if we are not under the influence of the Holy Spirit, we can't obey.

When we obey, the Spirit of Glory, the Holy Spirit, rests upon us. The Holy Spirit's purpose is to glorify the name of Jesus. (Romans 6:14, 8:11; 1 Peter 4:14) The same spirit that raised Jesus Christ from death to life will come to us when we obey the call of God on our lives. If we obey God's call in our weakness and foolishness, when we are despised, God will raise us up so that we can build other people's lives and be a blessing to them. Therefore, we need not be anything great. God tells us that not many mighty, noble or wise are called. He has chosen the foolish and the weak to bring glory to His name. (1 Corinthians 1:26-31)

All glory belongs to the Lord Jesus Christ. (1 Corinthians 1:29-30) We are not called to glorify ourselves. The Holy Spirit calls us to come and serve Jesus Christ, and all things will work together for good for those who are called by Him and love Him. (Romans 8:28) God is asking us to come, to draw near to Him; when we do, He will draw near to us. (James 4:8)

According to Romans 8:28, we are called according to His purpose, which gives our lives purpose. God called us when we were Gentiles with a purpose. (Romans 9:24) He called us to fellowship with Jesus Christ through the Holy Spirit alone. (1 Corinthians 1:9) God Almighty called us into the grace of our Lord Jesus Christ. (Galatians 1:6) We will be able to obey the call of God and receive the blessing of doing so only under the influence of the Holy Spirit. The Holy Spirit calls, "Come, as a bride prepared for the bridegroom. Make His name known to the nations." (Psalm 45:17)

Just like the Father and Son, the glory will be eternal. (John 17:22, Romans 8:21) Present suffering is worthwhile compared to the glory God will give us in the future. The

Apostle Paul, even though he suffered so many problems, still said, "Problems are momentary compared to the eternal weight of the glory." (2 Corinthians 4:17) Paul also admonished, in 2 Timothy 2:10, that we endure for the sake of the elect so that others may be saved with eternal glory. If we share in Christ's suffering, we also share in His glory. (1 Peter 5:1)

The Bible says in Isaiah 42:8, "I will not share my glory with another". Precious child of God, you are not "another" when you are under the influence of the Holy Spirit. The enemy is another. When the enemy is operating through our lives, we can also become "another", and God will not share His glory with us. Just as the Father, Son and Holy Spirit are one in the Heavens, when we join our spirit with the Lord, we become one spirit with God. (1 Corinthians 6:17) Then He shares His glory with us because we are one with Him.

God showed the biggest plan and destiny to Abraham. God said he would become a father to the multitude. Because Abraham believed, God counted him as righteous and fulfilled His destiny. (Genesis 15:6, Galatians 2:16) All the nations were blessed through him. God is not a respecter of persons. (Romans 2:11) What God did for Abraham, He will do for you. When you are under the influence of the Holy Spirit, that same God says, "Come towards your call; pursue God's destiny, and He will bless you."

CHAPTER SEVEN

Pray in the Spirit

When we pray to God, we can't see Him. No one can see God. No one has ever seen God, though some did see the Lord Jesus Christ. (John 1:18) When we pray, we don't hear an audible response from God.

If we are not influenced by the Holy Spirit, we can't pray what God intends or wants us to pray. Prayers that are not inspired by the Holy Spirit of God are short and very general—something like, "God bless me, my job, my business, and my family." When the Holy Spirit influences our prayers, those prayers become very effective.

Why?

Romans 8:26 tells us, "Likewise the Spirit also helps in our weaknesses: for we know not what we should pray, but the Spirit Himself makes intercession for us with groanings which cannot be uttered."

The Holy Spirit is known as our Helper. Jesus Christ told us in the New Testament that unless He departed, we wouldn't receive the Helper. (John 14:16, 26) God has given the Holy Spirit to help us in our infirmities. We have many weaknesses—both physical and spiritual. When we are physically tired, we don't feel like praying. When our spirit is oppressed with the cares of this world, we won't feel like praying. When the Holy Spirit influences us, we will be able to overcome these infirmities.

Jesus Christ was always filled with the Holy Spirit of God when He was on earth. When He met one woman who was bound by infirmity for eighteen years, He looked at her, called her, and laid His hand upon her. That woman, a daughter of Abraham, was set free; and all the people glorified the name of Jesus. (Luke 13:10-17) In the same way, God Almighty sends the Holy Spirit to deliver us from our infirmities, and in turn we will be able to deliver other people from their infirmities.

This is why we must seek the Holy Spirit's help when we pray. We must be careful not to grieve or quench the Holy Spirit with bad communication: bitterness, malice, clamor and evil. (Ephesians 4:29-31, I Thessalonians 5:19) The Holy Spirit, who dwells within us will intercede for us. The Holy Spirit knows past, present and future conditions. He will help us know what to pray. We must seek His help if we desire God's perfect will for our lives.

We see in James 5:16-18 that the fervent prayer of a righteous man avails much. Jesus Christ is righteous (Acts 3:14), and our Heavenly Father is the father of righteousness. (John 17:25) The Holy Spirit makes us righteous in the Kingdom of God. (Romans 14:17)

When we trust Jesus Christ who is righteous and believe He shed His blood for us on the cross, we are becoming righteous. (Romans 5:1, 7-8) When we have that righteousness and pray with the help of the Holy Spirit, our prayers will be powerful and bear much fruit. Consider Elijah, an ordinary man with a nature like ours. God sent down fire in response to Elijah's prayer. The God of Abraham, Isaac, and Israel helped Elijah when he prayed. (1 Kings 18:36-38)

Elijha prayed earnestly for it not to rain on the land, and no rain came for three and a half years in response to that prayer. He prayed again, Heaven gave rain, and the earth produced its fruit. (1 Kings 18:1-42) God commanded Elijah to pray like this because there was pride in the land due to their abundance, sinful living and idolatry. That is why God wanted to shut the heavens. God used Elijah, a man like you and me, to show a sinful people the error of their ways.

We must follow that pattern of Elijah, praying earnestly and continuously. That is why Jesus Christ commands us to pray without ceasing. (Luke 18:1) We must pray earnestly what God tells us to pray. To pray earnestly means that we are seeking what God wants us to pray. When that is our prayer, God will make it happen. Elijah prayed with that expectation, and his prayers were answered.

At one point, Elijah said, "I hear the abundance of the noise of rain." There was not a cloud in the sky—nothing to indicate that it would rain, but Elijah knew what God had said and trusted that God would send the rain. He put his head between his knees and prayed seven times. His servant saw a little palm-sized cloud during his seventh prayer. God sent the rain according to what He spoke. What is the beautiful thing we see here? When God sent the rain, the earth produced its fruit. When we see natural rain, sometimes it will destroy the crop. An unseasonal rain can destroy a crop. But when God gives the rain in due season according to His plan, it always bears fruit. God knows what time to give the rain to bring forth fruitfulness. (Genesis 8:22)

It is God's intent that our earnest prayers will bring forth fruitfulness all around us when we pray with the help of the Holy Spirit. Again, when we talk to God, we don't know what to pray without the Holy Spirit's influence. When we are physically weary, the Holy Spirit will recharge us. Similar to the way we charge a low battery on a mobile phone. To recharge our spiritual strength, we must speak in tongues with God because the Bible tells us, "A man who speaks in tongues is speaking to God." (1 Corinthians 14:2, 4) Speaking in unknown tongues edifies the church. (When there is no interpreter, you can speak directly to God. However, when you speak in church, an interpreter is needed.) We are not able to pray in tongues without the Holy Spirit, because the gift of tongues is the gift of grace from Almighty God, which involves the Spirit of Grace in our life. (1 Corinthians 12:8-10)

If we pray with our physical senses, the devil understands. However, when we pray in tongues, we are speaking directly to God and the devil cannot interpret what we are saying. When we are under the unction of the Holy Spirit, our prayers are directed and dictated by the Holy Spirit. We need not have any agenda.

The original apostles waited in one place on the Day of Pentecost for the Holy Spirit to arrive. (Acts 1:14, 2:4) They were all in one accord, and were filled with the Holy Spirit. They began to speak in other tongues as the Spirit gave them utterance. So the Holy Spirit gives utterance regarding what to pray and what to speak. You must understand that speaking in unknown tongues is not a matter of learning from someone; it is from the Holy Spirit. When you invite Him, He will help you.

Peter and the other apostles were uneducated and untrained people. (Acts 4:13) When they were filled with the Holy Spirit on the Day of Pentecost, they were able to speak in tongues. (Acts 2:16-28) The connection is beautiful when we direct our prayers with the help of the Holy Spirit.

When we pray in the Spirit, we will know the mind of the Holy Spirit who will witness to our spirit. (Romans 8:16, 1 Corinthians 14:13) Hence, we will become heirs with God, co-heirs with Jesus Christ when we are praying if we allow the Holy Spirit to join with our spirit. Then when the Holy Spirit prays, He will show us all of the things God has prepared for us. He will show us the deep things of God. Then we will see the manifestation take place. (1 Corinthians 2:9)

The influence of the Holy Spirit enables us to pray for a long time. Many people pray for only one or two minutes, directing their prayer only toward their needs. However, they cannot pray what God wants them to pray without the influence of the Holy Spirit.

In Mark 1:35, Jesus was our role model when He rose up early in the morning and went to a place of solitude. He started praying when no one else was present. He spoke directly to God, exactly what God wanted Him to pray. (Luke 6:12) At night, He also went to the mountains and prayed alone. Sometimes He prayed the whole night.

What did He pray?

He knew that He would die on the cross, and when He died that He must rise up. Only then would we become righteous. Only then would He dwell in our hearts as Lord and Savior. His ultimate intent was for all people to be saved.

This is why in the order of Melchisedec, when Jesus Christ was on earth, he prayed vehemently and cried tears for all of us because he was filled with the Holy Spirit. (Hebrews 5:7) This is why Jesus Christ was able to say, "The Spirit of the Lord is upon me. This day this Scripture is fulfilled." (Luke 4:18, 21) The Holy Spirit was continuously resting upon Him. May the same Holy Spirit rest upon us.

We see a man in the Bible named Jacob who, like Jesus, was able to direct his prayers throughout the whole night. He wanted to get rid of his old nature. He wanted to represent God. This is why he went to the river Jabbok. (In Hebrew this means the emptying place) He prayed and emptied himself. Jacob means "deceitful, cheater, supplanter, and heel grabber." But Jacob forsook his old nature, saying, "God, I don't want to be like this. What I desire is to be what You want me to become."

At this time he had wealth and everything else he could desire, but he had cheated his brother and his father, who was blind. He cheated his first wife, and he cheated his father-in-law. However, we see that God remembered the covenant He made with Abraham and then the vow He made with Isaac; God continued that everlasting covenant by making the confirmation with Jacob so that he became Israel. (1 Chronicles 16:15-21, Psalms 105:8-9)

We read in Genesis 32:22-28 the account of Jacob praying and wrestling with God. When God wanted to go, Jacob said, "No, not until you bless me." Then God asked him, "What is your name?" God knew Jacob's name when he was in the womb of his mother. At that time, God said the younger will rule the elder. God also said, "I love Jacob." It's obvious that God knew his name but that God asked Jacob this to see if he was willing to confess and forsake his old character.

Jacob replied, "Yes, I am a deceiver, supplanter, and heel grabber. My name is Jacob." Only then did Jacob see his true condition. He didn't want anything of the world. He wanted to depend upon God's leading by the Holy Spirit. This is what his blind father prayed in Genesis 27:27-28, "My son will be like the smell of the field."

What is that smell? Prayer. Prayer is like an incense. (Psalm 141:2)

God answered and made it real. Everything happened. God touched his pelvic bone. He limped the rest of this life toward the call, goal and direction of God. He became Israel. He went and blessed Pharaoh as an ordinary shepherd. (Genesis 47:7-9) When Pharaoh asked his age, he replied, "The years of my pilgrimage are 130 years. The rest of my life is short. I want to live for God." This is why we see in Genesis 49, when he blessed all twelve tribes, God honored that prayer of blessing.

When our prayers are directed by the Holy Spirit, God Almighty will make our prayers effective and fruitful like He did for Jesus Christ, Elijah and Jacob.

Our concentration increases when we pray in the Spirit. When we don't, our thoughts wander and our attention is diverted. (1 Corinthians 14:28) Moses prayed forty days and nights, all alone on Mount Sinai, and his face began to shine. Such a glory came upon him that the Israelites could not behold him. (Exodus 34:28, 29, 35) When we pray in the Spirit, we too will represent the image of God. This is what God originally intended for the life of human beings. (Genesis 1:26-27)

When we are influenced by the Holy Spirit, we will be thankful to God and to others who are helping us, such as employers, customers, or fellow Christians. A thankful attitude will be cultivated only when the Holy Spirit directs our prayers. Without His influence, we will have routine prayers and a thankful attitude never develops.

In Ezekiel 36:25-26, God said, "I will put a new spirit in your heart. I will give you a new heart; a heart of flesh." A heart of flesh means one that responds to the call and the needs of God and God's people.

King David was always thankful to God and to people. He was a man after God's own heart because the Holy Spirit was in his heart. (Acts 13:22) David said, "Oh my soul praise the Lord. All the things within me praise His Holy Name. Forget not all His benefits God has given. So that he will forgive your iniquity and heal your sickness." (Psalm 103:1-3) When we have a thankful attitude, God will always forgive our sins and heal our sickness—mind, body, soul and spirit. A thankful attitude will come only when we are speaking and praying in the Spirit. (1 Corinthians 14:17)

Praying in the Spirit results in a boldness and courage that shakes the devil's kingdom. (Acts 2:1-4, 4:29-31) The people were terrorizing the Apostles and threatening them not to speak in the name of Jesus. Then they all joined together in prayer, and the whole place shook.

Many people in the Bible who were influenced by the Holy Spirit were able to speak boldly. Ordinary people became extraordinary when they prayed in the Spirit. This is why King David had such boldness every time the Holy Spirit spoke through his mouth. (2 Samuel 23:2) David said, "My heart became hot within me. Fire burned within when I meditated upon the word of God. Then my tongue spoke." (Psalm 39:3)

Souls will be saved when we pray in the Spirit. God writes our names in the Book of Remembrance and will save us the same way He saved the house of Cornelius (Acts 10:4) Cornelius invited all of his relatives when Peter came to preach about Jesus Christ, and the Holy Spirit fell. Those Gentile people instantly received the Holy Spirit and began speaking in tongues and prophesying. This means that when God intended to declare His will towards men at that time, He made ordinary people able to speak in tongues. When our prayers are directed and influenced by the Holy Spirit, salvation results. (Acts 10:44-47)

When God speaks through us prophetically, others will be edified. (Acts 19:1-7, 2 Peter 1:21) When the disciples of John the Baptist met Paul, he asked them, "Are you baptized with the Holy Spirit?" They replied, "We have not heard of the Holy Spirit." When Paul laid his hands upon them, they were baptized in the Holy Spirit, received tongues and started prophesying. If we are not filled with the Holy Spirit, our prayers will be powerless. When our prayers are not directed by the Holy Spirit, sensual, earthly or devilish things will influence our prayers instead.

However, when our prayers are anointed by the Holy Spirit, they will be supernatural and God will give us supernatural ability and grace. Grace will always follow when we pray and will never depart all the days of our lives. King David said, "You anointed my head before my enemies, my cup runneth over."

What happened?

He said, "All the days of my life your grace and mercy shall follow me." (Psalm 23:5-6) We are enabled to speak God's plans and purpose when we pray under the influence of the Holy Spirit.

When we pray, we must let our minds think what the Holy Spirit wants us to think. God says His thoughts are higher, and his ways are higher than man's ways. His words never come back void—they perform the purpose for which they were sent. (Isaiah 55:8-9) The ability to pray without one word falling to the ground comes with the help of the Holy Spirit.

God always wants to honor us. That is why we must pray what God wants. 1 Corinthians 14:14 says, "For if I pray in an unknown tongue, my spirit prays, but my understanding is unfruitful." So the Holy Spirit is praying on our behalf; as a result, whether we understand or not, we will have God's plans, thoughts, ideas and mind when we pray. We will have the mind of Christ which is from above. (Colossians 3:1-2) When we pray under the influence of the Holy Spirit, God will honor our word and it will never come back void. Our counsel will be performed when we pray in the Holy Spirit. May God Almighty hear our prayers and give us fruitfulness.

CHAPTER EIGHT

The Holy Spirit Will Make Your Words Powerful

Jesus Christ boldly declared, "Heaven and earth shall pass away, but my words will never pass away." (Matthew 24:35) Where did this great confidence come from? Jesus had this great confidence because He was anointed by the Holy Spirit. The Spirit of the Lord was upon Him. (Luke 4:18-19; Isaiah 61:1-2)

Jesus proclaimed the Gospel to the poor, and through His words, the poor became rich. The blind received their sight, both physically and spiritually. He helped the orphans and the widows. He delivered people, like the man in Mark chapter 5, that were demon possessed. He encouraged people living in a disadvantaged condition and brought them into a place of advantage. He crowned the year with His goodness.

Again, Jesus confidently asserted, "Heaven and earth may pass away but my words will never pass away." He proclaimed, "The Spirit of the Lord is upon me. This saying is fulfilled in your hearing today." (Luke 4:21) Everyone was astonished by the words of grace that He spoke. (Luke 4:22) Everything he spoke came to pass. The same is true even today, because He is the same yesterday, today and forever. (Hebrews 13:8)

We should let the Spirit of the Lord be upon us too— upon our heart, our mouth and our tongue. When we are influenced by the Holy Spirit, we can speak like Jesus because our Lord Jesus Christ said, "Out of the abundance of the heart, the mouth speaks. A man out of his heart with good treasure speaks good things. A man out of the bad treasure in his heart speaks bad things." (Matthew 12:34-35)

This is why Jesus said, "The heart is the worst part of a man's life unless he is filled with the Holy Spirit." (Mark 7:21) Bitterness, jealousy, hatred, evil, wickedness, deception, cruelty, adultery and murder; all these things come from our heart. When our hearts are influenced by the Holy Spirit, when our mouth speaks, God will honor that word.

God said, "I will give you a new heart. I will put a new spirit in you. I will remove the heart of stone and give you a heart of flesh." (Ezekiel 36:25-26) A "heart of stone" means a stubborn attitude. The heart of stone does what it wants and refuses to react to the call of God. The heart of stone doesn't react to the needs of people. However, God, by His Spirit, will give us a heart of flesh.

When we speak from a place of brokenness and humility, even as a child, God will honor our words when they are influenced by the Holy Spirit. In the Bible, we see a boy named Samuel. He had other brothers and sisters, but he alone grew up in the presence of the Lord. (I Samuel 2:21) That is why he had favor before God and man. (I Samuel 2:26)

What is that favor?

Whenever Samuel spoke, not one word fell to the ground. (I Samuel 3:19) This means God honored his words. You must understand that we don't have a mouth so that we can speak whatever we want. We must allow God Almighty to speak to us. Then when we declare those words, we will see the power.

This is what King David spoke of in Psalm 62:11, "God spoke once. Twice I heard. The power belongs to God." What does this mean? Every word of Jesus Christ and God Almighty is powerful. God wants us to have the same power. God wants us to speak good words because life and death are in the power of the tongue. (Proverbs 18:21)

In Luke 4:22, people were astonished by the words of grace spoken by Jesus. When our words are influenced by the Holy Spirit, this same kind of amazement will be upon the people regarding us because Jesus said His words are life and spirit. (John 6:63)

Every religion claims to have a great book of teachings. How can we know our Bible is the greatest? The Bible is the only book that has life and spirit in it. What the Spirit Himself inspired was written in book form. (2 Timothy 3:16)

Today we must determine to let our words be influenced by the Holy Spirit. When we are willing to meditate upon what Jesus Christ said, we will speak in the same fashion. It is not us speaking, it is the Holy Spirit speaking through us. King David said, "My heart became hot within me. Fire burned within me." (Psalm 39:3, 2 Samuel 23:2) What is David speaking of? (Jeremiah 23:29) "His words are fire." This means when we have the zeal to see God's Kingdom established and we speak toward that end, God will honor our words.

When we speak words that are inspired by the Holy Spirit, people will be converted. When Peter was anointed by the Holy Spirit (Acts 2:1-4), not only was he able to prophesy (Acts 2:17-18), but when he told that crooked and evil generation to repent, 3,000 people gave their heart to Jesus Christ. God will give your words the same kind of power, which will convict people of their sin.

Our words must be truthful. The Word of God is Truth. (John 17:17) When the Word proceeds through our mouths truthfully, souls are won for God's Kingdom. May God Almighty anoint our words today.

Both Zechariah and the prophets spoke thousands of years ago about our Lord Jesus Christ. They spoke of how God Almighty would exalt the horn of King David. That horn is Jesus Christ Himself. (Luke 1:67-69; Psalm 132:17) Through our lives and words, God's words will be established. Speak what God has intended, and God will honor it. The Bible says, "If anyone speaks, let him speak the oracle of God." (1 Peter 4:11) We must go where God sends us, and say what He wants us to say, under the unction of the Holy Spirit. Then God will give us anointing without measure like Jesus Christ. (John 3:34)

We must allow God Almighty to touch our words and He will give us anointing without measure. This means, when you combine your gifting with prayer that is under the unction of the Holy Spirit, He will direct your words— "Jesus, let it be done for your people." Immediately the anointing without measure will come and many will be healed and delivered and will testify about God's grace.

Words anointed and directed by God are honored by God. We must let our words be directed under the influence of the Holy Spirit so they will perform the purpose for which they were given and never come back void. God wants to back up what we speak in the name of the Lord. He said He will hasten His word and it will happen when we release that word through our mouth. (Jeremiah 1:12)

Whenever our words are directed under the influence of the Holy Spirit, God will bring those words to pass. That is why God said, "Come to me, argue with me, prove you are righteous." (Isaiah 43:26) How can we argue with God, unless we base our argument upon the Word of God? When your words are backed by the Holy Spirit, God will accept them.

Let's say we pray for a barren woman. It's very easy to say that God will give a barren woman a child. (Psalm 113:9) Unless our words are anointed by the Holy Spirit and directed by the love of God, that barrenness cannot be removed. By His love, He will heal. (Deuteronomy 7:13-15)

We see in Acts 14:1-10 a man who was lame for forty years. Paul saw that the man had faith to be healed, so he commanded, "Stand on your feet." He did not even use the name of Jesus. Why? Because he was anointed by God. Paul said, "No more I live, Jesus Christ lives in me. The rest of the life I live, I live with faith in Jesus Christ." (Galatians 2:20)

What does this mean?

When Jesus Christ and His Word dwells in us, whatever we speak will happen. This is the kind of power your tongue can develop under the Spirit's influence. That is why God wants us to put His words in our mouths. He wants us to speak what He wants. We will have to give an account for every vain word, but every God-ordained word that we speak will be performed in our lives.

Our words carry such power. Use them for the glory of God.

CHAPTER NINE

Obey God's Commandments

God Almighty said, "I will give you a new heart. I will put my Spirit into you. I will remove the stone from your heart." (Ezekiel 36:26-27) The verse continues, "I will put my spirit in you and cause you to walk in my statutes. You will be careful to observe God's commandments and ordinances."

The influence of the Holy Spirit alone will help us to obey the commandments of God. Many times we want to obey God's Word when we go to church and hear the message, but later we do what we want instead of obeying. The Apostle Paul says, "What I want to do, I don't do. What I don't want to do, I do. What a wretched man I am." (Romans 7:21-24)

So, who can help?

The good influence of the Holy Spirit will help us. God said, "I will give you a new heart." A new heart does not mean physically cutting out our heart and giving us another—it means allowing the Holy Spirit to clean up the heart we have. Jeremiah 17:9 tells us that, above all, the heart is the most wicked part of the body.

In Mark 7:21-22, Jesus Christ said, "From within the heart the following things come that defile a man: evil, wickedness, adultery, fornication, lust, theft and murder." All the evil works that come out of the heart defile a man. In the New Testament, if you hate your brother (if you develop bitterness and hatred toward him), that itself is equal to murder. (1 John 3:15-16) The repercussion is that a murderer cannot inherit eternal life. (Revelation 21:8) So we must allow God to help us by the Holy Spirit to remove all these things from our hearts.

Jesus Christ said, "When I send you the Spirit of Truth, He will convict the world of sin, righteousness and judgement." (John 16:7-8) Unless we allow the Spirit to enter our hearts and help us, we will not be able to rid ourselves of these things or build up our relationship with God. Matthew 5:8 declares, "Blessed are the pure in heart for they shall see God." To see God means that God will reveal His plans and purposes. We will be able to see what God has in store for our lives through the inward eye of understanding of our heart. (Ephesians 1:17-18)

For that purpose, we need the Holy Spirit to help us get rid of the sin in our hearts. That sin grieves the Holy Spirit. (Ephesians 4:29-31) The Bible says we are to let no evil communication proceed out of our mouths.

How will evil proceed from our mouths?

Jesus said, "Out of the abundance of the heart the mouth speaks." (Matthew 12:34-35) A man brings good things out of his mouth from the good treasure in his heart. A man with bad treasure in his heart brings bad things out of his mouth (murder, theft, jealousy, clamor, stubbornness, bitterness and hatred). These all grieve the Holy Spirit. On one hand, we are defiling ourselves. On the other, we are grieving the Holy Spirit.

God Himself said, "I will give you a new heart. I will put a new spirit in you." He's not speaking of a human spirit, a spirit of the world. We need a new heart because what is in our heart is causing many of our struggles. We are exhorted to be careful about the different spirits in this world. (1 John 4:1) If we are not careful, we will not know which spirits have come into our hearts. We must allow God to put His Holy Spirit newness into our lives.

We see a great example in the story of King Saul. His deceitful mindset opened a door for the enemy to gain a foothold. Before he knew it, the enemy took full control of his life. God Almighty said to Saul, "Go kill all of the Amalekites, but don't take any of their property." But Saul brought back all of the fattened animals. When Samuel the prophet called him, Saul replied, "I spared the fattened animals because I want to sacrifice to our God." Samuel responded, in 1 Samuel 15:22-23, that obedience is better than sacrifice. He also said stubbornness is an idol equal to witchcraft.

Why did God instruct Saul not to spare anything alive?

In Exodus 17:14-15, God made clear His intention to completely wipe out the Amalekites to prevent them from fighting against His people from generation to generation. After 400 years of bondage, when the children of Israel were released out of Egypt to go through the wilderness to the Promised Land, the Amalekites tried to destroy the Israelites instead of welcoming them. Those people only gave trouble to God's children.

We see the same in Esther's time. Haman was an Amalekite. We also see in King David's time that the Amalekites attacked and took away the wives and children, then destroyed the city. (1 Samuel 30:1-19) That is why God wanted to wipe them out. This is why we all require the help of the Holy Spirit to obey God's call and meet the needs of the people.

God wants to give us a heart of flesh and a new spirit so that we will obey His commandments, His voice and His ordinances.

Why is this God's desire?

Obedience brings a blessing. Disobedience brings a curse. Satan wants us to disobey. The moment we disobey, the prince of the air is working through us. (Ephesians

2:2) The moment we obey, God's blessing will come. Even without our praying, God's blessing will fall upon us. (Deuteronomy 11:26-27; Deuteronomy 28:1-14) God said,

"This day if you hearken unto my voice, if you obey, I will set before you a blessing and a curse. If you will obey me, you will receive a blessing. If you disobey you will receive a curse." (Deuteronomy 30:19-20)

A curse means a constant pattern of the same difficulty, the same failure, the same nature of talking, the same nature of dubious character. That curse will pass from one generation to another as an inheritance, preventing what God intended to do to prosper us. Disobedience brings this curse.

God wants to give us a new spirit so that we will obey His commandments. The moment we obey, we become disciples of Jesus Christ. Only a true disciple is a Christian. (John 13:34-35; Acts 11:26) The first disciples in Antioch are known as Christians because of their obedience. We cannot simply say, "I am a Christian." We are Christians only when we obey, then we are true disciples of Jesus Christ. Only the Holy Spirit can give us the ability to obey God. The moment we start obeying God, we can claim all of His blessings. (Deuteronomy 28:1-14) It is not because of the law that God has given the blessing. God is giving the blessing for obedience.

Throughout Deuteronomy 28, God declares everything we set our hand to is a blessing. The fruit of our labor and righteousness, the fruit of our job or business and the fruit of our ministry will be blessed. The place where we live will be a blessing. God will make us the head and not the tail. He will set us above and not below. He will make us a lender and not a borrower. He will do this because we are called by His name, and we are a holy people. Enemies will fear us and flee away seven ways. These are all the blessings we will inherit the moment we obey and seek the help of Almighty God by the Holy Spirit to fill our hearts every day.

When we obey, we will not taste the curse. Consider Abraham. When God called Abraham, without knowing his destination, he simply obeyed God and went. (Hebrews 11:8-10, 13-16) He was living in a tent with the heirs of promise, but looking for a heavenly country whose builder and architect is God Himself. Because of that faith, God was not ashamed to be called his God.

If you ask someone who the President of the United States is, most people would know his name. If you ask the President of the United States if he recognized the name of most people in America, he would not. Similarly, many say, "Jesus is my God." But Jesus must be able to acknowledge that we are His people.

Our hearts will be filled with the Holy Spirit by His help. We will be directed by the Spirit to avoid pursuing our own desires that will cause us to fall into the trap of the enemy. Only the Holy Spirit can help us to fulfill the desire of God and do what pleases Him.

The God of Glory appeared to Abraham and blessed him. (Acts 7:2) Who is this God of Glory? The Spirit of Glory that has raised Jesus Christ from death to life, the same Spirit of Glory will help us to live a glorious life. That is the Holy Spirit experience. (Romans 6:4) He will lift us up. (1 Peter 4:14) When the Spirit of Glory comes upon our flesh, we will be refreshed and will become glorious people in this generation. Now the Lord is the Spirit. Where the Spirit of the Lord is, there is freedom. (2 Corinthians 3:17-18)

God will take us from glory to glory—not gloom to glory or dust to glory. He is the Spirit. It will be a spiritual experience. You must accept the help of the Holy Spirit to be able to obey. We can be blessed in the same way that our father Abraham was blessed.

When God called Abraham, his father was an idol worshipper, but when God called, He gave Abraham a tremendous blessing. (Joshua 24:3-4) God said, "Abraham, I will bless you and make you a great nation. I will make your name great. You shall be a blessing. All the families of the earth will be blessed through you. Whosoever blesses you will be blessed and whosoever curses you will be cursed." (Genesis 12:2-3)

This became the first Gospel. (Galatians 3:8) Here we see what happened next. (Galatians 3:13, 14, 16, 29) We all became entitled. God removed the curse of the law. He gave us the blessing of Abraham. Not only the children of Abraham (the Jewish people), but also the Gentiles who believe and trust in Jesus are entitled to the same blessing. This is why you must allow the Holy Spirit to work in your heart, to remove the heart of stone and give you a heart of flesh so that you will respond to the call and goal of God.

We see how father Abraham went forth in a powerful way with nothing but God Almighty beside him. (Genesis 30:2) There was not a place to contain all that he had been given.

Why did that happen?

Abraham gave the tithe. God blessed him because the lesser is blessed by the better. The living one, Jesus Christ, takes the tithe, and we are blessed. (Hebrews 7:6-8) That is why God made Abraham exceedingly rich. (Genesis 24:35) Due to his obedience, God said, "You, your children and generation, like sand on the earth and stars in the heaven I will multiply. For I know you fear me. You have not even withheld your son to offer as a sacrifice on the altar." (Genesis 22:12-17)

Many people in the Bible who obeyed God were blessed: Abel, Enoch, Noah, Abraham, Isaac, Jacob, Sarah, David, and Paul. All these people obeyed God and were automatically blessed. Obedience will come only when the new spirit comes. Otherwise, it is not possible. In our life, we must be willing to obey God with the help of the Holy Spirit.

CHAPTER TEN

The Holy Spirit's Gifts and Abilities

The Apostle Paul said, "Stir up the gifts that are within you." (1 Timothy 1:6) When God created us, He gave each of us certain abilities. When we are born again by His grace, we are given certain gifts, talents and abilities. If we do not stir up these gifts with the help of the Holy Spirit, we will never realize whether a gifting is there or not.

For example, a piece of coal is red and beautiful when it is burning. However, once the fire goes out, ash slowly forms on the outside of the coal. Even though there might still be fire inside, it can't be seen because of the ashes. If you stir the coals and knock off the dead ash, the fire becomes visible again. Even the smallest fire in a piece of coal has the potential to burn down an entire forest.

So how can the Holy Spirit be stirred up?

The Word of God is like that fire burning deep inside the coal. That is why God said, "Is not my word like fire." (Jeremiah 23:9) When we are cold-hearted, we are like those cold ashes. We think to ourselves, "Where is God? What is happening?" (Jeremiah 5:12) We can even be attending church regularly and still be cold-hearted. That's when we need to stir up the Holy Spirit.

In Genesis 1:2-3, a deep darkness was hovering upon the waters. The Holy Spirit hovered over it.

Why does the Holy Spirit have to hover over it? What is this deep darkness? What are these waters?

In Revelations 17:15, the Bible tells us the waters are adulterous women who sat on the waters. The waters represent multitudes, nations, different tongues, while an adulterous woman represents being cold-hearted, or the works of the flesh. If the Holy Spirit does not hover over us or stir us up, we will never be able to see the light of God. When the Holy Spirit was hovering over the waters, only then was God able to say, "Let there be light." Then there was light.

Without the help of the Holy Spirit, God, Jehovah Himself, could not do this. The earth was formless and void because Satan and one-third of the angels had fallen down. The entire world was in chaos. There was no creation. The entire world was destroyed, full of waters. The waters were full of darkness. Darkness was the constant state. (Deuteronomy 28:29)

God had pity on us because we are all His children, and He wants us to walk in the light. That light is Jesus Christ Himself. (John 1:4, John 8:12, 1 John 1:5-7) This is why it is important to be stirred up by the Holy Spirit in order to achieve everything that God wants you to do.

The term to "stir up" means again and again; when we speak about it, we will automatically be prone to walk in that. If we speak continuously about the gift of the Holy Spirit and the fruit of the Holy Spirit, the Holy Spirit will automatically help us.

For example, if we constantly speak about immorality, anyone listening will be inclined to indulge in immorality. If we speak constantly about food, listeners will want to eat. If we speak about politics, we will stir that up and people will be interested in politics. If we constantly speak lies, they will soon appear to be true. Anything that we stir up again and again, we and those hearing us will be inclined to go in that direction. Therefore when we stir up the gifts and abilities that God gave us, that will become our direction.

God has prepared everything for us before the foundation of the world. (Ephesians 1:4) In the moment that we choose to love God, we will be able to see what God prepared for us. If we don't love God, we will only be able to see the natural man. Only the Holy Spirit is able to show us the gifts and abilities God has prepared for us. (1 Corinthians 2:9) That is why it is important to have the influence of the Holy Spirit.

The Bible says, "If anyone speaks, let him speak the oracle of God. If anyone does ministry, let him do it according to the ability that God has supplied." (1 Peter 4:11) We cannot do ministry beyond the ability that God has given, which means we will not fully use God's given ability if we are not stirred up by the Holy Spirit.

God has given nine gifts of the Holy Spirit. Some gifts are given the moment we are born again. (1 Corinthians 12:8-10, 28) We must be prepared to stir up those gifts. Unless you are hungry for God's righteousness, you cannot stir them up. When we are satiated, we are stagnant—there is no room in our hearts for God. A river where the water is flowing is continuously fresh, but stagnant water becomes dirty and smells.

When the Holy Spirit stirs us up, we will be fresh. When we are in a satisfied or stagnant state, God cannot do anything with our lives. If a glass is full of water, how can you add more? Only when a glass is empty can you fill it.

Every day, whatever ability God has given us, we must use it so that we can be filled over and over again. When we stir up the Holy Spirit, living water will flow out of our lives. Our life will be such a blessing. Jesus Christ said, "Whoever is hungry and thirsty, come unto me. I will give them living water. Living water will flow through the heart and belly." (John 7:37-38) We must have this kind of hunger for the Holy Spirit so that our life will become a blessing and, in turn, we will make other people's lives a blessing.

We must hunger after righteousness, not self-righteousness. Someone might say, "I am a spiritual man." He might even wear a white robe or suit. This is worldly righteousness. In the sight of the Lord, our righteousness is like filthy rags. God does not want that kind of righteousness. We must thirst after the righteous ways of the Lord.

Matthew 5:6 says, "Blessed are those who hunger and thirst after righteousness: for they shall be filled." We can be filled only when we are hungry for righteousness. (John 17:25) Our Father is the father of righteousness, and Jesus Christ is also holy and righteous. (Acts 3:14) The Holy Spirit imputes that righteousness in our life because we are trusting in the Father and the Son.

When we pray for others and bless people, our gift is getting discharged. Then when we are stirred up in the Holy Spirit again, we are being recharged the way we charge a battery on a cell phone. If we have a gift and don't use it, we are like the ash-covered coal. We must ask the Holy Spirit to stir us up and then wait upon God. He will send the Holy Spirit to help us and give us strength. Jesus Christ told us, when we ask the Father for the Holy Spirit, He is willing to give us what we seek. (Luke 11:13) This means we must constantly ask the Holy Spirit to stir up our gifts and abilities. When we ask, He will do that, because Jesus Christ came into this world in order to baptize us with the Holy Spirit and fire. (Matthew 3:11)

When the Holy Spirit arrives, will we have power. (Acts 1:8) When the Holy Spirit is stirred up, healing will take place if we ask for it. Otherwise, the healing gift might be in us, but remains dormant.

Sometimes, our unbelief hinders us. "If I pray and the person doesn't get healed, they may think I am a phony." Or we might think, "When I pray, they may think I have no gifting if there is no healing." We may be condemning ourselves instead of allowing the Holy Spirit to help stir us up.

Unbelief renders our gifts idle. An idle man may think about getting something from the Lord, but it will never happen. That is why it is important to ask and pray regularly. Note that wherever God sent Jesus Christ, He went. What God wanted Him to speak, He spoke. Therefore God gave Him the anointing without measure. (John 3:34) Are we willing to be led by the Holy Spirit and go where the Spirit takes us? Only then, will we be known as the sons and daughters of God. (Romans 8:14)

We see in Ezekiel 47:1-12 that water came into the temple. It touched the ankles, knees, waist, neck and then Ezekiel had the swimming experience. He swam in the knowledge of God. If you are satisfied with the ankle experience, you will not experience the water touching your knees. Only the swimming experience must satisfy you, accept nothing less.

When the waters flowed out of the river to the ocean, all the dead things in the sea came back to life. The bitter and salty water became sweet. When we constantly stir up the gifts of the Holy Spirit deeper and deeper, year by year, we will grow in the call of God and our lives will be a blessing. Wherever we go, our gifts and abilities will operate naturally. People's lives will be transformed. People will be blessed, and because life came to them through your word and gifting, they will bless you.

We must be stirred up in the Holy Spirit so that we can rise up and build God's kingdom. Otherwise, our viewpoint will be through the eyes of the natural man, and we will consider people useless. Zerubbabel was a governor who received no help from the people. Everyone was building their own houses and doing their own thing. Discouraged by this, he thought, "God told me to build. How can I do it?"

One day the Spirit of the Lord spoke through Haggai, "Zerubbabel, do not fear. I will make you a signet in my hand." This means "I am giving you authority." Where does this authority come from? The moment you realize you are sealed by the Holy Spirit, you will have the authority. (2 Corinthians 1:20-21) In the old days, if a seal was put on an ordinance, the entire country would follow and obey. God will bless us the same way.

The word of God came to Zechariah with this message: "Tell to Zerubbabel, Not by might, nor by power, but by my Spirit, says the Lord. Oh mountain what are you before Zerubbabel? Zerubbabel will carry the cap stone. All the people will say grace and grace and grace unto it." (Zechariah 4:6-10)

What is that grace?

When the people "say grace," the Spirit of Grace is stirred up. Otherwise they would simply be quiet and stand. (Zechariah 12:10, Hebrews 10:29, Hebrews 12:15) When the Spirit of Grace is stirred up, impossible things become possible. The gifts are the grace. The moment he started building, Zerubbabel laid the cornerstone and the temple was built. That is why the thread and the plumb line in the hand of Zerubbabel was watched by seven eyes. The seven eyes are the seven spirits of God, the seven spirits that were upon Jesus Christ. (Isaiah 11:2)

God wants to put the same spirits upon us, these are: Spirit of the Lord, Wisdom, Counsel, Knowledge, Understanding, Might, and the Spirit of the Fear of the Lord. Jesus Christ was constantly praying and seeking the Father. That is why every day He was filled with the Holy Spirit.

Since we are also in this world, we must pray and stir up the Holy Spirit within us. If we don't stir ourselves up in the Holy Spirit, the enemy will stir up against us. When stirred up, we will boldly speak what God wants us to speak and the enemy will be defeated. All the enemies were saying to the apostles, "Don't speak in the name of Jesus." What did they do? They went, prayed and asked for the Holy Spirit. They said, "God, we want to speak boldly in Your name. Send your Holy Spirit." As a result, they were all filled with the Holy Spirit, and the place started shaking. They spoke boldly from that day. (Acts 4:29-31) We must continuously pray, asking for the Holy Spirit to stir up our gifts.

Our prayers will rise like an incense before God. It is no use to simply burn incense; when the air and wind comes, the beautiful smell will spread. The Bible tells us about a sinful woman who brought an alabaster flask of perfume to Jesus. You can't smell the perfume in a closed bottle, but smell comes out the moment you open the lid. That is why this woman broke the bottle—the entire room became fragrant. Her act became a silent prayer. (Luke 7:37-50) Allow the Holy Spirit to come, and your prayers will be like an incense in the sight of the Lord. Your life will become a sweet aroma to the saved, and a sweet smell to the perishing people. (2 Corinthians 2:14-16)

When the Holy Spirit stirs us, we will be able to sing songs. Song of Solomon 2:14 says, "You are my dove flying in the cleft of the rock. Your voice is melodious." Our voices will be melodious only when we are stirred up in the Holy Spirit in the midst of difficult times. Paul was in prison, his hands and feet chained. This is the time he stirred himself up in the Holy Spirit and started singing, praising and worshiping the Lord. The moment he was stirred up, God shook the prison, opened the doors and Paul was sent forth in freedom. (Acts 16:25-31) This is why Ephesians 5:18-20 says, don't be drunk with wine. Speak, sing, make melodies and songs in your heart, then God will bless you. Then give thanks to God in the name of Jesus.

When we are stirred up in the Holy Spirit and the fear of God comes, our life, family and generation will be blessed. We must stir up the Spirit of the Fear of the

Lord. Otherwise, after a period of time, we will lose the fear of the Lord. We begin to think anything that we do is okay, but we must always be mindful that Jesus Christ is with us.

If we could actually see Him, would we dare to do some of the things we do?

He is the King of kings and the Lord of lords. All of the people and the apostles in heaven fall prostrate before Him. They are not even able to stand in His presence. (Revelations 4:11) Today, we are extremely casual before Jesus. We must honor Jesus Christ. In our life we must be able to stir up the Spirit of Fear of the Lord. Then God will do good to us. He won't stop doing good. He delights in doing good. All the good that He promised, He will bring it to pass when we stir up the Spirit of the Fear of the Lord.

Jesus always feared the Father. Jesus said in John 5:19, 30, "What my Father sees, I see. What my Father speaks, I hear. I fear my Father. Without him I can't do anything." Because of that fear of God (not fear of Satan), God won't stop doing good to us. The upright man fears God. (Proverbs 14:2) When we are righteous, God won't withhold any good thing from us. (Psalm 84:11) We must walk like Jesus Christ and humble ourselves, then God will bless our lives.

Today we may be small, but when the Spirit of the Fear of the Lord comes, God will make us great. (Psalm 115:13) When we fear God, He will send His angels all around us. (Psalm 34:7) Job feared God. Even though he underwent tremendous difficulties, God gave him a double blessing in the end. (Job 1:1, 8; 42:1-2) Every day we must stir up the Spirit of the Fear of the Lord. We mustn't fear the devil. We mustn't fear man. We must fear Almighty God and humble ourselves under His mighty hand; then God will exalt us.

CHAPTER ELEVEN

The Holy Spirit Will Help Us in Our Marriage and Family

King David said, "Lord, teach me to do your will. Lead me unto the land of your plain by your good spirit." (Psalm 143:10) When the Good Spirit comes, He will influence every area of our lives. In 2 Samuel 7:25-29, we hear the prayer of David:

> *"Now, oh Lord, the word which you have spoken concerning your servant and his house; establish it forever. Do as you have said. Let your name be magnified forever, saying, 'The Lord of Hosts is the God over Israel,' and let the house of your servant David be established before you. For you, O Lord of Hosts, God of Israel have revealed this to your servant. Saying, 'I will build you a house.' Therefore, your servant has*

*found it in his heart to pray this prayer to you. And
now, O Lord God, you are God and your words are
true. You have promised this goodness to your servant.
Now therefore let it please you to bless the house of
your servant that it may continue before You forever.
For you, O Lord God, have spoken it and with your
blessing let the house of your servant be blessed forever."*

This is how God Almighty wants to bless us. The Holy
Spirit influence in our life will give us the grace to hate
divorce and hold on to family values. We see God's heart
regarding divorce in His Word.

> *"Yet you say for what reason? Because the Lord has
> been witness between you and the wife of your youth
> with whom you have dealt treacherously. Yet she is your
> companion and your wife by covenant. But did he not
> make them one, having a remnant of the spirit? And
> why one? He seeks godly offspring. Therefore take heed
> to your spirit and no one deal treacherously with the
> wife of his youth. For the Lord God of Israel says that he
> hates divorce for it covers one's garment with violence.
> Says the Lord God of hosts, 'Therefore take heed to your
> spirit, that you do not deal treacherously." (Malachi 2:14)*

God Almighty wants to help us preserve our family
values and keep our families together. This requires the
help of the Holy Spirit. No one in the world is without
challenges, but God Almighty will help because He has
been a witness between you and the wife of your youth.
God is saying He is a witness of your marriage and mar-

riage is the covenant of God. When God establishes a covenant, He does not break it. (Psalm 89:34) He said, "My covenant I will not break nor alter the words that have gone out of my lips."

God Almighty wants to help, prosper and bless our lives. That is why, as God is the witness, his covenant is for a thousand generations. (Psalm 105:8-9) We can hold onto the blessing when we hold onto the covenant of God, the One who won't break the covenant. God has given a wife as a companion by covenant.

Did he not make the husband and wife as one? Why did God make them as one flesh? (Genesis 2:18-24)

He makes two as one flesh having a remnant of the Spirit so that only by the Spirit can we hold together as one flesh. Without the influence of the Holy Spirit, the husband and wife will become two separate beings, and conflict will result.

God made spouses one flesh because He wants godly offspring. God does not want us to join our bodies with others and get children the way we want. For His sake, He wants to bring godly children through the marital relationship. Therefore, in our homes, we must take heed to our spirit. We must join our spirit with the Holy Spirit to become one with the Lord's Spirit. (1 Corinthians 6:17) "Let none deal treacherously with the wife of his youth for the Lord God of Israel says that he hates divorce. For it covers one's garment with violence, says the Lord of Hosts."(Malachi 2:16)

See to your spirit that you do not "deal treacherously" means when we are under the influence of the Holy Spirit, we will desire to hold fast to our marriage as a covenant and God will bless us. Proverbs 20:27 says, "The spirit of a man is the lamp of the Lord searching all of the inner depths of his heart." So God Almighty has given us the spirit of our Lord Jesus Christ as a lamp searching all the inner depths of our hearts. God Almighty wants to bless us, our family and our generations. Only when we give room to the Holy Spirit can He hold us together. If there is no influence of the Holy Spirit, marriages will be broken and divorce will ensue.

Everywhere in the world, you can see that the divorce rate is increasing. It is not because of the culture. It is not because of emotions. It is because people are not heeding God's Spirit. When we give room to God's Spirit, we are made able to overlook wrongs. When we hold onto God's covenant, we may experience difficult times, but the covenant of God will never break. The Bible tells us it is impossible for God to lie by two immutable things. (Hebrews 6:18)

What are the two immutable things?

One is God's promise, representing His truthfulness. The other is His covenant, representing His faithfulness.

God said He made one flesh, and He wants to raise up the children as a godly generation. Despite problems and difficult emotions, every time we yield our human spirit to the Holy Spirit, He will help us and bring a beautiful family out of our surrender. When Samuel anointed King David, the Spirit of the Lord came upon him in a very beautiful way. (1 Samuel 16:13)

After he killed Goliath, King Saul gave David his daughter to wed in order to keep his promise. Saul became jealous and began chasing David to harm him, and he had to run for his life, leaving his wife behind. Saul gave Michal to marry another, but David maintained a constant spirit. Even after he married other wives, he gave an opportunity for Michal to come back and kept her as a wife.

What happened?

Since there was no spirit in her, she despised him. She said, "How glorious was the king of Israel today. Covering and uncovering himself in the eyes of the maids of the servants, as a base fellow (vain) shamelessly uncovers himself. Therefore Michal the daughter of Saul had no children unto the day of her death." (2 Samuel 6:22-23) Even if we already have children, the moment we allow thoughts like these, we become unfruitful.

The first thing God wants us to do is follow His commandments to, "Love the Lord God with all our heart, soul, and strength. As well, love your neighbor as yourself." (Matthew 22:37-38) He wants us to take care of our family. (1 Timothy 5:7-8) God said, "If anyone doesn't take care of his family, he is worse than an infidel."

God allows divorce for three reasons—adultery, domestic violence, or when one partner wants to serve the

Lord and the other is obstructing. Other than these, God Almighty wants us to hold dear the relationship between husband and wife. King David prayed a very important prayer before the Lord in 2 Samuel 7:25-29. "Now oh Lord God, the word which you have spoken concerning your servant and his house establish it forever and do as you have said." So God alone is able to establish our family and our house. For that, what we need is wisdom from Heaven.

This is what the Bible says in Proverbs 24:3-4. "Upon wisdom, the house is built." That wisdom is from Heaven. (James 3:17) That kind of wisdom is what both the husband and wife must seek from God. We see in Deuteronomy 34:9 that Joshua received the Spirit of Wisdom. That is why he said in Joshua 24:15, "As for me and my house we will serve the Lord." In the same way, women must also have the Spirit of the Lord. Proverbs 14:1 declares, "A wise woman will build her house." Ultimately everything revolves around the wisdom of God.

God is Truth; He cannot lie. We must trust Him one-hundred percent for His wisdom. Marriage counselors, lawyers and judges will always give one-sided advice. It may please the husband or the wife, but rarely will such advice bring reconciliation. Even if it does, the same issues will soon arise again. In contrast, when the Holy Spirit deals with a couple, conviction will come and a beautiful reconciliation will develop. A couple led by the Holy Spirit will cherish their marriage and household, and it will continue until the Lord Jesus Christ comes or until they go to Heaven—whichever comes first.

What God says, He will do. He alone can establish us. When God establishes something; no one can shake it. (2 Samuel 7:26) David said, "So let your name be magnified forever." God wants our relationships to be very glorious so that our family will bring glory and magnify the name of the Lord. God wants our families to be role model families. A husband and wife can be enabled through the Holy Spirit to glorify Almighty God in body and spirit. (1 Corinthians 6:19-20)

The Heavenly Father's name will be glorified through a marriage yielded to Him, and that couple will bear much fruit. As Christians, whatever our difficulties, we must not look unto the difficulty. Instead, we should seek to glorify God and know that He will work all things together for good. (Romans 8:28, Matthew 5:16, John 15:8) We must always seek to magnify God's name. The moment we magnify the Lord, wherever we are, and wherever our family is, God Himself will come and bless us. (Exodus 20:24)

In Ruth chapter 4, the elders at the gate were talking about Ruth, a Moabite woman. Moabites were a cursed generation. For ten generations they could not enter into the assembly of God. However, God Almighty turned the curse into a blessing. (Deuteronomy 23:5) These elders said, "This Ruth is not ordinary. Ruth will build the house of Israel in the same way Rachel and Leah did."

Even though Ruth came from a cursed generation, she married Boaz. Boaz begot Obed, Obed begot Jesse and Jesse begat David. Through David's lineage, Jesus Christ was born. (Matthew 1:1, Luke 1:3-5) What the elders said came to pass. Whenever you take the name of the God of Israel, His name is so powerful that it will start building your family. God will build your family and you will magnify the name of God. King David said in 2 Samuel 7:26, "And let the house of your servant David be established before you."

Building is one thing. Establishing is another. That is why Proverbs 24:3-4 says, "Upon wisdom let it be built. But upon understanding let it be established." Even though God has given us wisdom, sometimes we are not able to understand that wisdom. This is why God will give us not only wisdom, but also understanding. Understanding is implementation of the wisdom that God has shown. As an example, we see in Exodus 31:1-5 that God not only put His Spirit in Bezaleel, but He also gave him a Spirit of Wisdom and the skill to understand. He showed him how to convert wisdom to understanding. We must ask for the Spirit of Understanding so that our families will be established.

Under the covenant, God blessed Abraham. After Abraham's death, his son Isaac was automatically blessed. (Genesis 25:11) The same God will help us and our children by doing good. Jeremiah said, "Under the everlasting covenant, He (God) won't stop doing good." The same way that God made an everlasting covenant with Israel, He also made an everlasting covenant with King David.

You are living under the same covenant today, and God will bless you. (Isaiah 55:3, 1 Chronicles 16:15-21) Trust in that covenant. What God promises, He will do because He is a good God. Just as our Father God is good, Jesus Christ is also good and will do good unto our lives. He never intends bad things for anyone. When Jesus Christ was sojourning on this earth, He went around doing good to people, healing the sick and delivering the captives. (Acts 10:38) Trust our good God, Jehovah. Trust our good God, Jesus Christ. Whatever goodness God has promised you, surely God will do good to you as you are influenced by the Holy Spirit. King David said, "Now therefore let it please you to bless the house of your servant."

When we please God, He wants to bless us and reward our life. It is impossible to please God without having faith in the Son of God, Jesus Christ. (Hebrews 11:6) Build up your faith in Jesus Christ, and you will please God. Today God wants to bless your house, marriage and family. Obey and yield to the Holy Spirit, and the Holy Spirit will guide you. This is why King David was able to say, "All the days of my life I want one thing, to be in your holy presence." (Psalm 27:4)

Why is he saying, "Let my house continue in your holy presence"?

The moment the presence of God comes, we will be delivered from the snare of the enemy. (Psalm 31:20) Our family will be established, and we will have the joy of the Lord. (Psalm 16:4) The moment His presence goes before us, all obstructions will be removed, and He will give us rest. (Micah 2:13, Exodus 33:14)

When He is present, He will also give us honor and prosperity. (1 Chronicles 16:27) That is why God Almighty wants our house to be established before His presence forever. King David said, "Oh Lord God, you have spoken, and with your blessing let the house of your servant be blessed forever." God wants our family and our generation to be blessed forever—not just for one generation.

Many times people get weary and tired after one month of marriage and they become just one of many divorces. Couples become weary in life. When we accept the help of the Holy Spirit, we will hate divorce and teach our children that God who makes the covenant will not break it. Our intention must be to hold onto family values.

A successful marriage is not about attending counseling or seminars. The Holy Spirit presence is able to envelop us and bring the greatest unity to our relationships. The moment we decide to live in unity, it is His responsibility to pour out His spirit and anointing upon our families. It is then His responsibility to command His blessing upon us from Mt. Zion, like dew from Mt. Hermon. This is why we must decide today to live in unity with our families. (Psalm 133:1-3) Seek the good influence of the Holy Spirit. All the crooked paths will be made straight. He will take us unto the plain. Seek the help of the influence of the Holy Spirit.

CHAPTER TWELVE

Freely We Give

As a pastor, without the influence of the Holy Spirit, even if you continuously tell the people your needs, there may be no provision. But when you and the people are under the influence of the Holy Spirit, giving happens without putting forth any effort.

We have to remember that building God's Kingdom is not for our sake. It is for God, and for His Spirit to dwell in. God Almighty wants to dwell along with us and to move with us. That is His basic desire. In both the Old Testament and the New, we see the places where God walked in the midst of His children. (Deuteronomy 23:14, Exodus 29:45, Revelation 1:20, Revelation 2:1) We are the dwelling place of God. (Ephesians 2:22) That is why to build God's Kingdom, we want to either give resources or receive them from God's people (as a pastor.) The key to giving is when people are influenced by the Holy Spirit;

then giving is very easy as Spirit-filled people are always willing to do what God commands.

Those who are not under the influence of the Holy Spirit attribute a request to give as a desire of man to manipulate others for his own gain.. We see in Exodus 35:4, 20 and 21 that Moses the prophet spoke to all of the congregation of the children of Israel, saying, "This is the thing which the Lord commanded, Take from among you an offering for the Lord." Moses is telling the children of Israel two things: 1) This is what the Lord commanded. 2) The Lord commanded me to take the offering.

As long as giving is the Lord's commandment, and He is saying to take an offering in order to build His temple, the response will be tremendous. As representatives and ambassadors for God, as well as new creations, it is our responsibility to simply tell about the needs when God tells us to build up His Kingdom. (2 Corinthians 5:17-20)

The moment Moses shared the big list of needs in Exodus 35:6-19, even with such a large need, the people were willing. They were not fed up. Generally if one pastor shares all of the needs (for the poor, missionary work, church construction, etc.), people can get fed up. They don't even feel like going to church. When Moses asked, he was talking about gold, silver, precious stones, wood, copper and iron. So much was needed in order to build the tabernacle for God. All of the children de-parted after hearing from Moses. They departed from the presence of Moses, but they did not depart from the presence of God. But God's Spirit through the words that

Moses spoke did not die or leave the people because Jesus Christ said in John 6:63, "My words are life and spirit." People need the vision and presence of God, not the manipulation of man.

We come to the key in Exodus 35:25, which says, "Then everyone came whose hearts were stirred up and they brought the Lord's offering for the work of the tabernacle, of the meeting for all of the service, and for the holy garment." Many hearts were moved and stirred up by the Spirit of God, and all of the people were willing to give.

We see another example in 2 Chronicles 36:22 in a Gentile man named Cyrus. God said, "Cyrus is my shepherd whom I have chosen. Who will do all my will. He is my anointed one; I will go before him. All the crooked places I will make straight. I will cut off the chains of iron, the gates of bronze and I will give the treasures of darkness. I will give the riches from the hidden places." (Isaiah 45:1-3) The crooked places are created by Satan. That is why he is known as the crooked serpent. (Isaiah 27:1)

Why did God Almighty give the treasure of darkness, the riches from the hidden places?

Here is the secret: When God stirred up the spirit of Cyrus, he said, "I am going to give all of the resources that God has given in order to build the temple for the children of Israel." So he prepared all of the resources that were needed for God's plans and purposes. He is a Gentile man, but God Almighty chose him. According to Jewish tradition, Jews would refuse to take anything from the Gentiles. The disciples who became Apostles refused to take from the Gentiles. (3 John 1:7) It could have happened the same way. So you must understand this is what God did. (Ezra 1:1, 5-11) God not only stirred up the spirit of Cyrus, He also stirred up the spirit of the tribes of Judah and Benjamin in order to build the temple. Even if one man's heart is stirred up, if the other people do not cooperate, it is of no use. What God Almighty prepared for Himself, He also prepared the people to use for His glory. When the people brought the offering, they brought it cheerfully because the Holy Spirit moved. Only when the Holy Spirit moves upon our spirit and heart will we give cheerfully. The people gave cheerfully because their hearts and spirits were stirred up by the Holy Spirit. Paul says, "Whosoever brings the offering to God let him give it cheerfully. God will bless a cheerful giver." (2 Corinthians 9:7)

We must ask ourselves, "What is the obstruction?" Sometimes God blesses, but there is an obstruction that makes us unwilling to give. However, God not only gives us riches but at the same time will stir our hearts, enabling us to give. He will do both when he stirs up our heart and spirit through the Spirit of God.

When we are moved by the Holy Spirit, we will give what God says. We will do it obediently, not as a legalist. God will multiply our resources when we give out of obedience. When Abraham gave, he was nothing. He had nothing. He was lonely. Yet God made him a role model. That is why God said, "Look unto your father Abraham, and your mother Sarah. When they were alone, I called them, blessed them, and multiplied them." (Isaiah 51:2) The same God is going to multiply you when your heart is moved and you are stirred by the Holy Spirit. Abraham gave to the God who is living; His name is Jesus Christ.

When we give to the living God, miracles and multiplication will happen through our hand in the same way. God said in Deuteronomy 28:1-8, "When you obey, I will bless the fruit of your hand and the fruit of your labor." We see in Mark 6:41-42 over five thousand hungry people (men, women and children); they had nothing. But one boy had five loaves and two fish, and the disciples brought it to Jesus. He asked the people to sit down, then He looked to Heaven, prayed, blessed it, and gave it into the hands of the disciples. As they started serving it, that food started multiplying in the hands of the disciples— not in the hands of our Lord Jesus Christ. When you are moved by the Spirit to give and place your offering into the hands of Jesus Christ and say, "Lord, I'm giving this offering, this tithe, to You, into Your hand, not the hand of any man," God Almighty will bless, and multiplication will happen because it is in the hand of the Lord.

We will become the planting of the Lord. (Isaiah 61:3, Jeremiah 32:41) When the Lord plants, He doesn't plant in an ordinary way. When He plants, surely He will give a thousand-fold growth. Every effort we put forth will be successful. That is why we must allow the Holy Spirit to stir us up and move on our spirit so that we will know where to give, when to give and how to give. What God said is real. What God promised, He will return back. He will reward us. This is the confidence we must have.

CHAPTER THIRTEEN

Love Your Enemies

The Holy Spirit influence helps us to love those whom it is very difficult to love, and we will receive a blessing from Heaven when we do. Paul said in Romans 15:30, "Now I beg you brethren in the love of Jesus Christ and through the love of the Spirit that you strive together with me in prayers to God for me." This means, we need to look at people through the lens of the love of Jesus and the Spirit, instead of looking through the eyes of our natural flesh.

Without love, we have no God. 1 John 3:15-16 says, "If you hate your brother and do not love him you are equal to murderers. No murderer will inherit eternal life." On the contrary, murderers are destined to go to hell. (Revelation 21:8) That is why the choice is very clear. We must decide to follow God. As God is love, we must walk in the love of God under the influence of the Holy Spirit. (1 John 4:8) Love is greater than everything. (1 Corinthians 13:13) When you are under the good influence of the Holy Spirit, even the most unlovable people that have done wrong to you, who hated you, who are not worthy to be loved—you will be in a position to love under the influence of the Holy Spirit.

It is hard for us to comprehend how God Almighty is able to love even the worst criminals—thieves, murderers, adulterers, abominable people and sinners. Romans 5:8 says, "God demonstrated his love for us. While we were still sinners, He died for us." God will give us the same kind of heart to love others when we are under the influence of the Holy Spirit, because love is a commandment of God.

Paul explains how the Spirit of Love works in Romans 5:3-5, "Tribulation produces patience, patience produces examination, examination produces hope. Now hope does not disappoint because the love of God has been poured out in our hearts by the Holy Spirit who is given to us." Without the love that is poured out by the Holy Spirit, we will not be able to transition from tribulation to hope, nor will we be able to love others - even our enemies.

When God pours His love into our hearts through the Holy Spirit, our hope never disappoints. The first thing Paul explains in Romans 5:3-5 is tribulation. Our Lord Jesus Christ said, "In this world you will have tribulation, but be of good cheer for I have overcome the world." (John 16:33) The Apostle Paul said, "It is with much tribulation that we shall be able to inherit the kingdom of God." (Acts 14:22)

The meaning of the kingdom is described in Romans 14:17—"The kingdom of Heaven is not a matter of eating or drinking, it is a matter of love, joy, peace, and righteousness in the Holy Spirit." Whenever we have tribulation, yet still walk in the love of God and forgive people, we will receive the supernatural ability to love the most unlovable. God is able to change the circumstances in our lives. Paul said, "When my outward man perishes, my inward man is renewed, for the weight of the glory makes all the problems lighter." (2 Corinthians 4:16-17)

We must understand that our forefather Abraham underwent great tribulation. In Genesis 20, King Abimelech took Abraham's wife captive to marry her. However, God Almighty intervened and said to King Abimelech, "Abraham is my prophet. Leave his wife. He will pray for you." God left the choice to Abraham to obey and pray, or fight in the natural. True prophets are always directed and moved by the Holy Spirit. (2 Peter 1:21) The prophets always faced tribulation, but God was with them.

So here Abraham's wife was taken captive, which was a tremendous tribulation in his life. When God told Abraham to pray for his enemy, you can imagine His internal struggle. He was a warrior whose tendency would have been to fight. Yet, God is asking him to pray. He obeyed God. He forgave his enemy and prayed for the household, and all the women who were barren were able to conceive children. (Genesis 20:1, 17-18) God not only delivered Sarah from captivity, but He also removed her barrenness and gave the promised child, Isaac. (Genesis 21:1-4)

Many times in our lives, the fulfillment of God's promise comes immediately after a significant decision to obey. When we choose to love instead of hate, in the midst of tribulation, God will bless us. We must not develop bitterness or we will grieve the Holy Spirit. (Ephesians 4:29-31) If we have bitterness towards others, grace will depart from our lives. (Hebrews 12:15) This is why we must all be willing to forgive.

In the tribulation period of his life, Abraham forgave. God will also give us the supernatural ability to forgive. If we regard the sin and iniquity in our hearts, God won't hear our prayers. The fact that God heard the prayers of Abraham meant he had no bitterness in his heart. He forgave them. The influence of the Holy Spirit will give us supernatural ability to forgive.

Even in tribulation we will be able to inherit what the Kingdom of Heaven has for us. We must remember that tribulation produces patience. When we are under the love of God, love is patient. (1 Corinthians 13:7-13) The Bible says, "Blessed are the people who are patient." God has compassion on those who are patient. We have all heard about the patience of Job. (James 5:11) We see the patience in his life when Job lost his ten children and all of his property. (Job 1:1, 8; 2:1-4) Job was a blameless man who shunned evil and feared God. He was an upright man with great character. However, Satan came to kill, steal and destroy. (John 10:10) Job lost his seven sons and three daughters. He lost his property when fire came. Then he lost his health. When he turned to his friends and his wife, their attitude was ruthless. They scoffed at him. (Job 2:9, 16:20-21, 19:17, 19) Job's wife said, "Why don't you curse your God and die?" His friends were scornful, commenting against him. However, in the midst of all of this, Job had patience, waited on the Lord and did not speak hastily. He said, "I know my redeemer lives. I will see Him with my own eyes." (Job 19:25) Then he said, "God, You can do all things. Your plans and purposes shall never be defeated." (Job 42:2) God's purpose was not defeated because Job had patience, and God showed compassion.

We get compassion not because we earn it, but because of God's mercy. (Romans 9:16) In the midst of tribulation, Abraham was able to forgive the enemy because he possessed the love of God. In the midst of many problems, Job had patience; so he was able to forgive his friends who scoffed at him and eventually offer a burnt sacrifice on their behalf. What a great and unique opportunity.

When we have that kind of patience, what happens?

Job became exceedingly rich and got a double blessing. He had ten more children. Afterward he lived one hundred and forty years and saw three to four generations of his descendants. (Job 42:10-12)

Patience produces examination. Sometimes, God wants to test us. He doesn't tempt us. God tests us to promote us, the devil tempts us to demote us. After Abraham received the promised child, Isaac, God said, "Abraham, take your son Isaac and offer him as a sacrifice." (Genesis 22:1-12) So Abraham took fire, wood and knife up to Mount Moriah. He told his servants, "Wait here while we go to the mountain to worship and come back." Isaac asked, "Father, there is fire and wood, but where is the lamb for the sacrifice?" This is when Abraham replied, "God will provide." (That is why God is known as Jehovah-Jireh, the Lord who provides.)

When there is an exam and we pass, God will provide the blessing for us and for our generation. God said to Abraham, "Like sand on the seashore and the stars in the sky, I will bless you." God made a vow to Abraham and fulfilled it. Passing God's test, Abraham received back his son Isaac, and the generations were blessed through one man. That is why tribulation produces patience, patience produces examination, and examination produces hope.

When we have hope only in God—and not in any fleshly man—our hope will never disappoint. Jeremiah 17:5-8 says, "Cursed is the man who trusts in the flesh. Even when good things come around him, he can't see. (Because he is under a bad influence, like the leaven of the Pharisees.) But the people who hope and trust in God alone will be like a tree planted by a river of water whose roots grow deep. Even in the hot season, the leaves will be green. Even in drought, the tree will not stop bearing fruit."

Throughout our life we must only hope in the living God because Jesus Christ is our living hope. (Romans 15:13) Hope in our Lord Jesus Christ will never put us to shame. That is the confidence we must have.

When the Spirit of Love is upon us, we are under the influence of the Holy Spirit. God Almighty promises to turn our curse into a blessing because of His love. (Deuteronomy 23:5) When that love is upon our life, we have the ability to overcome every curse.

Curses vary. If our forefathers worshipped idols, we have a curse for three and four generations. (Exodus 20:6) When we disobey the voice and Word of God, we get the curse through the prince of the air. (Ephesians 2:2) Some curses are self-imposed, that is why the Bible says, "Life and death are in the power of the tongue." (Proverbs 18:21) Rebecca said to Isaac, "Marry any of these country girls and it is better that I die." Her words were a self-imposed curse. He married the country girls, and Rebecca died before Isaac.

In the same way, we see Jacob as head of the family, when he was leaving his father-in-law, Laban, said, "If anyone stole the idols from my father-in-law, let them die." He did not know his wife had taken her father's idols. It was a human-imposed curse. When we are under the influence of the Holy Spirit and are filled with the love of God, we have the power to condemn any curse or witchcraft, because it is our heritage that no weapon formed against us shall prosper. (Isaiah 54:17)

In our life, we must look to God and walk under the influence of the Spirit of Love to overcome curses that would bring us harm. When we realize how God loves us, we will become very fruitful. God will remove all the barrenness and deathly sickness. (Deuteronomy 7:13-15) We must believe we have a supernatural ability to love when we are under the influence of the Holy Spirit. We will be able to love even our worst enemies. We will not nurse bitterness and grieve the Holy Spirit. We will serve as role models representing the love of God to the world. The Apostle Paul said, "The love of Christ constrains me." (2 Corinthians 5:14) Before Paul was saved, he was filled with hate. (Acts 8:1-5, 9:1-6; 1 Timothy 1:15) Paul was the chief sinner and persecuted the church beyond measure. The moment he was filled with the Holy Spirit, the goodness of God's love was evident.

Without the love of God in our hearts, we will not be able to see God's plans and purpose. When under this kind of influence of the Holy Spirit, not only will we love our fellow human beings, but we will also love our God. Under that love, God will show the things He has prepared for us before the foundation of the world. Until this time, what our eyes have not seen, what our ears have not heard, what our hearts have not perceived, God will be able to show us. (1 Corinthians 2:9)

Not only was Paul converted, he became a powerful chief apostle who proclaimed the Gospel because of this love. He carried an anointing so heavy, that even his handkerchief healed the sick. (Acts 19:11-12) We see how our forefathers—Paul, Abraham and Job—walked in love. As a result, God did wonders, signs and miracles through them so Gentiles would be subject to the Gospel. Do not walk under the influence of the devil with hatred. Decide today to walk under the influence of the Holy Spirit, the Spirit of Love.

CHAPTER FOURTEEN

Spirit of Love

Only when we are under the influence of the Holy Spirit can we follow God Almighty and love Him fully. Sometimes Christians go to church, and sometimes they don't. Some days they pray, and some days they don't. Some days they read the Bible, and some days they don't. Then when they have troubles, they ask God, "Why did this happen?" When they experience problems, they backslide. People are easily offended and then refuse to go to church.

However, when we live under the influence of the Holy Spirit, the Good Spirit of God, we are able to follow God and love Him fully. In Matthew 22:37-38, God commanded, "Love the Lord God with all your heart, with all your soul, with all your strength; love your neighbor as yourself." To fully follow God like this requires the Good Spirit of God.

God gave a promise to Father Abraham regarding the children of Israel.

"Your generation will go to a country they do not know. They will be slaves for four hundred years. But then I will visit them and I will bring them out with a multiplication and an abundance of blessing." (gold, silver, cattle, etc.) (Genesis 15:20)

God said it, and God did it. God brought the children of Israel out of Egypt as the passover lamb was slain. That passover lamb was the Lord Jesus Christ. From the foundations of the world, He died for us. (Revelation 13:8, Exodus 12)

When the children of Israel came to the wilderness, they simply had to trust the promise of God. God's promise never fails. He is not a liar. What He says, He will do. (1 Kings 8:56, Numbers 23:19) God made a covenant with Abraham, renewed the vow with Issac and gave the confirmation to Jacob.

God said, "I will take you to a land flowing with milk and honey...What I promised to your forefathers, Abraham, Isaac and Jacob, under that covenant. I will deliver you, bless you, and take you to the promised land." (Psalm 105:8-9)

However, the moment the Israelites came to the wilderness, they went to Moses and said, "Send some of the men to the land God promised. Let them go and see how the people are there, and how the crops are, and whether or not milk and honey are flowing." This itself was not God's desire. God wants us to be like little children. God wants us to believe and have faith in what He has promised. (Mark 11:24) Instead of having simple faith, the children of Israel wanted to find out what the country was like before they went, but this was their own heart's desire.

Many times we are enticed by our own heart's desire. (James 1:14) When we get entangled in seeking that, we lose our direction and focus. God Almighty said to Moses, "Send them, one person from each tribe to spy out the land. It is not the plan of God. It is the heart's desire and the plan of human beings." (Numbers 13:1) Ten spies from ten tribes came back with a bad report. They said, "We look like grasshoppers in their sight and in our sight also." Hearing this, the people were distraught, crying and broken. "Why did God bring us here?" They started murmuring against God.

The man Caleb had a different report to give. "Let us go up at once. We are able to overcome." (Numbers 14:24) Only he and Joshua gave a favorable report. "We can go to the promised land because God said it. We trust that God will help us." God witnessed the faith of these two men and said, "My servant Caleb has a different spirit in him and has followed me fully. I will bring him and his descendants into the land and they will inherit it." When you have a different spirit—a spirit of love—you will follow God fully, not half-heartedly. You will love God fully, not half-heartedly. Because of his faith, Caleb received the reward. He got to go to the Promised Land, and his descendants inherited that land.

Exactly as God promised, Joshua became the leader in place of Moses because Joshua served Moses for forty years. When Moses was on Mount Sinai, Joshua waited below faithfully. What God commanded, Moses obeyed. What Moses commanded, Joshua obeyed. (Joshua 11:15) Because of that, he became a leader. God's promise is always fulfilled. Joshua said to Caleb, "You know the word the Lord said to Moses... He told the Israelites, 'you shall by no means enter the land which I swore I would make you to dwell in.'" (Joshua 14:6/Numbers 14:30)

What we should notice is that God gave the biggest inheritance to Caleb, which was the land Hebron. When Caleb was forty, he started serving Moses. At eighty-five, he had the same strength that he had when he entered the Promised Land. When we follow God Almighty fully, He will give us that same kind of strength. (Deuteronomy 1:36) God said, "To Caleb and his children, I am giving the land because he wholly followed the Lord." When we follow God with our whole heart, He will give us the blessing. (Joshua 14:6-15) God will fulfill His every plan and purpose. Only with the help of the good influence of the Holy Spirit are we able to fully follow the Lord. Whatever our difficulty, trouble or tribulation, we must follow the Lord God fully. Determine today to follow Him with the help of the Holy Spirit.

CHAPTER FIFTEEN

Follow Your Mentors

Psalm 143:10 is a good passage for meditation.

"God teach me to do your will. You're my God. By your good spirit make me to walk in the land of the plain. Make straight all the crooked ways and the rugged paths created by the enemy."

When we are under the good influence of the Holy Spirit, we can walk in a level and plain land. The Holy Spirit influence will encourage us to walk with anointed people and seek mentors who can guide our lives.

The Bible says in Proverbs 27:10 and 17, "In your day of trouble better to go to a friend than your family members because.... As iron sharpens iron a true friend sharpens the countenance of his friend." We also see that, "A true friend loves all the time." (Proverbs 17:17) We must understand that we will have fellowship with other anointed people only when we are also under the anointing of God. Then we can live as Jesus Christ did.

In the Old Testament, the Bible shows us examples of the influence anointed people will have on us, and the influence we will have on others by walking in the Spirit.

In 2 King 2:1-15, Elisha showed perseverance and dedication to pursue Elijah and insist that he be his mentor. Before Elijah was to be taken to Heaven, he instructed Elisha to stay behind while he went to Gilgal, Bethel, Jericho and crossed the Jordan. Each time Elijah instructed Elisha to remain behind, he responded, "Surely as the Lord lives and you live, I will not leave you."

Elisha recognized the anointing and power Elijah obtained from God. Before Elijah was taken to Heaven, he asked, "What can I do for you before I go?"

Elisha responded, "I want a double portion."

Elijah answered, "What you ask is difficult, but if you see me go, you will have what you asked for." Elijah's response meant that if Elisha wanted the same anointing, he needed to keep his eyes on him at all times, not missing anything he said or did.

His request was granted and Elisha received the double anointing of his mentor, Elijah.

As an aside, I've learned this lesson from the Holy Spirit. We need not ask for a double portion like Elisha asked of Elijah. This is the Old Testament and would actually limit God. Since we are in the New Testament time of grace, thanks to Jesus, we can ask God for "anointing without measure."

Similarly, Joshua inherited the same leadership and power transferred to him from Moses. In their time, Moses was surrounded by thousands of people whom he loved, yet he only fellowshipped with Joshua. Moses said, "One will drive a thousand. Two will drive ten thousand." He knew authentic fellowship with another can expand God's kingdom further then walking alone.

In another example, King David was anointed by God to lead Israel. He had almost six hundred people around him who were murmuring, indebted, discontented, poverty-ridden people. However, when David became king, he made them commanders, rulers and helpers. Being around the anointed king made a difference in their lives as they emulated his character and heart. In the same way, when we follow anointed mentors, our lives will be impacted.

When we are in proximity to and moving with anointed people, our lives will be altogether changed. John the apostle was very close to Jesus and wrote of his experience how his anointing and fellowship with Jesus made his life totally different than the other apostles. He said:

"That which was from the beginning, that which we have heard, that which we have seen with our eyes, which we have looked upon, and our hands have handled, concerning the Word of life (and the life was manifested and we have seen, and bear witness, and declare unto you the life, the eternal life, which was with the Father, and was manifested to us), that which we have seen and heard declare we unto you also, that you also may have fellowship with us, and truly our fellowship is with the Father, and with his Son, Jesus Christ." (1 John 1:1-3)

That is why our fellowship with anointed people will "rub off" and our level of anointing will multiply.

Let's examine several of John's statements:

"That which was from the beginning..."

"In the beginning was the Word, the Word was with God, and the Word was God." (John 1:1) This is why Jesus Christ is known as the Alpha and the Omega. (Revelation 21:6, 22:13)

"Which we have heard."

So they heard about Jesus Christ. John, because he was so close to Jesus, even in the midst of tribulation on the Isle of Patmos when he was in the spirit, heard the voice of God like a trumpet. (Revelation 1:10) Without the influence of the Holy Spirit, he could not have heard the voice of God.

"Which we have seen with our eyes."

Unless God opens our spiritual and inward eyes, we cannot see His plans and purpose. God Almighty, Jesus Christ alone must help us see. Peter said, "He has not been seen by all, but some of the witnesses who were with Jesus, who ate with him, only those saw him." (Acts 10:41-42)

"Which we have looked upon and whom we have handled."

John the Apostle leaned on the chest of Jesus Christ concerning the Word of life. John 1:4 says "In his Word there is life. That life is a light unto the people." Let us not miss this Word of life. When we believe Jesus Christ under the influence of the Holy Spirit, we believe these words of Jesus when He said, "My words are life and spirit." (John 6:63) That's why they are words of life. Jesus said in John 14:19 "As I live, you also live." Only when our words are anointed by the Holy Spirit do they become the words of Life.

When Peter was delivered from the prison by the angel of God, the angel said, "Go and speak the words of this Life." The words of this Life are Jesus Christ. (Acts 5:20) So John had such a close fellowship with Jesus that he was able to get the revelation of Jesus Christ. (Revelation 1:1) This happened despite the fact that he was an uneducated man. (Acts 4:13) This close fellowship with Jesus is why he was able to dictate the vision he received and write the book of Revelation.

When we have fellowship with the Light, God will sanctify us with His Blood. (1 John 1:7) God Almighty anointed John with the good influence of the Holy Spirit, and the words of Life came out. So in our life we must move with anointed people—not with those who murmur or gossip. When we walk with those who are murmurers and gossips, we also begin to murmur, judge and gossip—then we will not achieve anything.

When we have fellowship with anointed people, they will impart good into our lives. Moses laid his hand on Joshua, and not only did Joshua receive the Spirit of Wisdom, but the people also obeyed Joshua in the same way they obeyed Moses while he was alive. (Deuteronomy 34:9-10)

Paul had great fellowship with Timothy. He considered him as a son. When Paul laid his hands on Timothy, Timothy received the gifts. (2 Timothy 1:6) Paul, said, "Stir up the gifts you received when I laid my hand on you." We must understand how important it is to move with anointed people so that the good presence in them will multiply our blessings in every area of life. This is how we must think so that our lives will shine.

Daniel 12:3 says, "Faces of the wise will shine like the firmament of Heaven. Whoever turns many to the righteousness of God they shall shine like the stars in the heavens." This experience comes only when we have fellowship with anointed people.

We love everyone, but we need not have fellowship with everyone. It is better to be in a right relationship with a few anointed people, than have fellowship with many. In our lives, we must search to get the right people around us, and the Holy Spirit will help us.

We must imitate the people who are led by the Spirit. Paul said in 1 Corinthians 11:1, "As I imitate Christ, imitate me." In response to our prayers, God will show us who is genuinely walking in the footsteps of Jesus. (1 Peter 2:21) Those are the people we must definitely follow without equivocation to receive blessings from God Almighty. May God Almighty multiply our anointing as we walk with anointed people.

CHAPTER SIXTEEN

Fullness of Joy

When you are under the influence of the Holy Spirit you will have fullness of joy, and God will restore the joy of your salvation. The Bible says in Psalm 16:11, "You show me the path of life. In your presence is fullness of joy. At your right hand are pleasures forever." King David said, "Restore to me the joy of your salvation and uphold me by your generous spirit." (Psalm 51:12) It is impossible to restore joy or to have the fullness of joy without the presence of the Holy Spirit in our lives.

Who is this King David in the Bible? Let's look at his life and how God restored the joy of his salvation.

When Saul, the first King of Israel, was anointed by Samuel the prophet, God put His spirit upon him. Saul became a completely different person. He went to search for donkeys, but returned a king and became a prophet. (1 Samuel 10:6) God chose Saul to be king in order to destroy the Amalekites who fought with the children of Israel when they came out of bondage. After four hundred years of bondage in Egypt, they were delivered and were on their way to the Promised Land.

The Amalekites fought with the Israelites instead of helping them and God was angry. Moses lifted his hand, Joshua fought, and they were victorious. That is why God is called Jehovah-Nissi. (Exodus 17:15) God Almighty said, "Generation to generation I have the fight with the Amalekites."

So God said to Saul, "Go and kill all of the Amalekites, the king, soldiers, households and the animals. They are all cursed. Don't bring anything with you out of their land." However, Saul did not kill the king, some of the people, and the animals. When he returned from the battle, he justified his actions when Samuel the prophet questioned him: "I brought this back to give God an offering." Then God's word came, "Obedience is better than sacrifice." (1 Samuel 15:22-23)

According to this passage, rebellion and deceit are equal to witchcraft and idol worship (rebellion against God). As a result of his disobedience, God rejected Saul. Then God's word came to Samuel, "Go to the house of Jesse. Anoint one of his sons to be the ruler over this nation."

Samuel went and spoke to Jesse who brought seven of his sons before Samuel, one at a time. Each time, God said, "No... Man sees the face (the outside) but I see the heart." (1 Samuel 16:7) Samuel finally asked Jesse, "Do you have any other sons?" Jesse replied, "I have an eighth son who is an ordinary shepherd. He is in the field."

Seven of the sons were at home when Samuel came. This means that they were loiterers, lazy and did not work. They may have been proud and spiteful. God did not choose them. Instead, the humble shepherd boy was the one God anointed. David was only seventeen years old when God chose him and Samuel anointed him. From that day onward, the Holy Spirit was upon David with fullness of power and might. (1 Samuel 16:13)

Later, David fought Goliath who was threatening the children of Israel. David said, "You come against me with the spear and sword, but I come against you in the name of the God of Israel." He took the sling and five small stones into that battle and hit Goliath, who was ten feet tall, on the forehead. The giant fell down and died, but it was not the stone and sling that killed him. It was the Holy Spirit who went before David and destroyed the enemy. (1 Samuel 17:45)

Later, by compulsion and out of fear, Saul gave his daughter as a wife for David. When the people said, "One thousand praises to Saul. Ten thousand praises to David," Saul became jealous and thought that David might one day take over his kingdom. Out of that fear, he planned to kill David. When David found out, he ran away to the wilderness. Once his journey began, he experienced sorrow after sorrow, and problem after problem. Remember that even though Saul had given his daughter Michal to David, when David left, Saul wickedly gave Michal to marry another man.

Try to imagine the young man, David. His first marriage was a failure. He was running for his life and being chased by King Saul for five years. Finally he had to hide in enemy territory.

It is inevitable that we will all come to a crossroads or a turning point in life more than once. What was David's turning point?

We see it in 1 Samuel 30:1-19. David and his men went out and then came back only to find that the Amalekites had burned their houses and stolen their wives, children and possessions. All of the people wept, including David, and all his men wanted to kill him. They felt they were facing this devastation because of him.

Only the anointing of the Holy Spirit can break the yoke. (Isaiah 10:27) King David looked unto God who strengthened his heart. David inquired of God and God said, "Pursue the enemy. You will recover everything." He obeyed and was able to destroy the enemy and recover everything, just as God said. In all of our lives, God wants to bless us. The wealth of the wicked is stored for the righteous. (Proverbs 13:22)

After the death of Saul, David became King of Judah at twenty-three years of age. At age thirty, he became King of Israel.

So why was David saying in Psalm 51, "God, restore the joy of my salvation"? What happened?

We see the background in 2 Samuel 12:1-15. After David committed adultery with Bathsheba, the prophet Nathan came and spoke a parable to David. He said:

"There is a rich man in our city. He has large flocks of sheep, goats, and cows. He had a neighbor who is very poor who had only one lamb. This poor family loved this lamb. It ate and drank with them. They treated it like their own daughter. But one day some guests came to this rich man, and he took the poor man's lamb and served it to his guests for dinner."

Hearing this, King David immediately became angry and said, "Who is that man? He should not live. He must be killed. Whatever that poor man lost, he must be repaid fourfold." Nathan responded, "It is you who did this wickedness."

Immediately, King David cried and repented, "I sinned against God. I sinned against Heaven." This is when David wrote Psalm 51. In verse 12, he begged God, "Restore to me the joy of my salvation. Uphold me in your generous spirit."

God's generous spirit alone will uphold us. Many times, new children of God are so hungry for God and full of the joy of our salvation. We go to prayer meetings. We fast, pray and tell people we meet that we have accepted Jesus. But as the years pass, we sometimes come to the place where we don't even know how long it has been since we have laughed wholeheartedly—since our joy has been full. Our hearts are crushed in the busyness of life. We have lost our joy—but joy comes when sinners repent. (Luke 15:7-10) For that reason, let's consider what King David is expressing, point by point.

Psalm 51:1 : "Have mercy upon me, O God, according to your loving kindness, according to the multitude of your tender mercies."

When we want the restoration of joy, it means restoration of the Holy Spirit in our lives. We must always come not by trusting our righteousness, but by trusting the mercy of God. (Daniel 9:18) God is a merciful father whose mercy is for a thousand generations. He will never forsake us. (Deuteronomy 4:31, 5:10, 2 Corinthians 1:3)

In the same way, Jesus Christ is the merciful son of God. (Matthew 14:14, 15:32) Every time Jesus Christ has mercy and compassion on people, the Heavenly Father also has mercy and compassion. In order to restore the joy of your salvation, come unto God and ask for mercy. His mercy will take away your cry and lamentation. (Philippians 2:27)

When mercy comes, you need not run continuously in order to achieve so many goals in your life. Mercy will give you everything you need. Romans 9:16 says, not because of our will or because we run, but because of His mercy. That is why King David said, "O God, have mercy upon me."

Psalm 51:2 – "Wash me thoroughly from my iniquity and cleanse me from my sin."

Because of our iniquity, God is hiding his face. But when we forsake that iniquity, God heals us and we obtain His mercy. (Isaiah 59:2; Psalm 103:3) The joy of our salvation is restored. Only then will the Holy Spirit come into your life.

Psalm 51:3 – "For I acknowledge my transgression and my sin is always before me."

When we lose the joy of our salvation, our sin will always be in front of us. We will always think about the transgression. But the good news is that Jesus Christ died for our iniquity and transgressions. He is wounded and bruised for us. By his stripes we are healed. (Isaiah 53:5) Jesus said in Isaiah 43:25 and Hebrews 8:12, "No more will I remember your sin and iniquity." What a great, wonderful and merciful God we have! Come to that God. Put your burdens and transgressions upon Jesus Christ and have the joy of your salvation restored with the help of the Holy Spirit.

Psalm 51:4 - "Against you only have I sinned and done this great evil in your sight, so that You may be found just and blameless when You judge."

When we are sinning, we are not sinning against just anyone, but against God Himself. When we want to restore the joy of our salvation, we have an advocate, Jesus Christ, who will argue on our behalf. (1 John 2:1)

Psalm 51:5 – "Behold I was brought forth in iniquity and in sin my mother conceived me."

Sin passes from generation to generation. It is there even from the time we are in our mother's womb. As an example, we see Jacob and Esau. Jacob grabbed the heel of his brother Esau at birth when they were in Rebecca's womb. This type of sin comes from birth, so many are losing the joy of their salvation. We must come to Jesus who can anoint us with the Holy Spirit and fire so that once again we receive the joy of our salvation.

Psalm 51:6 – "Behold You desire truth in the inward parts (the hidden parts); You will make me know wisdom."

When one commits the sin of adultery, he lacks wisdom and understanding. (Proverbs 6:32) That is why we must come back to God who can give us wisdom, because Jesus Christ is wisdom. (1 Corinthians 1:24, 30) "All wisdom is hidden in Christ Jesus." (Colossians 2:3) By wisdom, we will overcome the lust of the flesh and come into the joy of salvation. Wisdom that comes from Heaven is pure, peaceful, willing to yield, merciful, fruit bearing, impartial and without hypocrisy. (James 3:17)

Psalm 51:8 – "Make me hear joy and gladness so that the bones that you have broken may rejoice."

Here we see joy and gladness. It is the voice of the bridegroom called Jesus Christ, who alone will bring gladness.

Psalm 51:9 – "Hide your face from my sins and blot out all of my iniquities."

That is why he wrote Psalm 32:1, which says, "Blessed is the one whose sins and iniquities are blotted out and covered by Almighty God." God alone is able to restore the joy of our salvation with the help of the Holy Spirit.

Psalm 51:10 – "Create a clean heart, oh God, and renew a steadfast spirit in me."

Having a clean heart again requires the help of the Holy Spirit. In Ezekiel 36:25-26, God said, "I clean you with my clean waters. I put my spirit in you. I give you a new heart, a heart of flesh." That is why in our life we have to ask God to give us a new heart, a clean heart, and a heart of flesh that responds to the call of the God and the needs of people. It is not selfish. Instead of going to war, King David's heart was on the lust of flesh. He said, "Renew a steadfast spirit in me." Our spirit needs continual renewing. That is why the Apostle Paul said in 2 Corinthians 4:16-17, "My inward man is renewed day by day, though my outward man perishes." Even if our outward man perishes, we want to renew in our inward man day by day. Only God can do this kind of renewal. It will happen only if God renews and revives. (Psalm 85:6)

Psalm 51:11 - "Do not cast me away from your presence, and do not take your Holy Spirit from me."

King David knew the value of God's presence. He said in Psalm 27:8-10, "When my father and mother leave me, You will draw me. You told me to seek Your face, to seek

Your presence. I am here." In Psalm 27:4 he said, "All the days of my life I seek only one thing. That I may dwell in the house of the Lord forever." He was seeking the Presence of God.

We have to clearly understand God's plan for our lives. Without the Holy Spirit's presence, we will dry up like a fish out of water who dies from lack of air. Like the fish who thrives when surrounded by water, we must seek to be submerged in the Holy Spirit's presence for survival. God's presence fills the heavens and the earth. (Jeremiah 23:23-24) Unless we are filled with the power of the Holy Spirit and the presence of God, we can't become great people, but the presence of God will make us exceedingly great. (Psalm 21:6) His presence brings us honor and glory. (1 Corinthians 6:20)

So in every area of life, we need the presence of God twenty-four hours a day. That is why David said, "Do not take your Holy Spirit from me." If the Holy Spirit departs, we will dry up; we will be useless and lose the purpose God has for our lives.

In Judges chapters 14-16 we read about Sampson, whom God chose and raised up as a judge with great strength in order to destroy the Philistines. For twenty years, Samson ruled well—then he committed adultery with Delilah. When this happened and the Philistines came to bind him, he wanted to rise up like other times with the power of the Holy Spirit to kill the enemy. Judges 14 and 15 tells of his great strength. He killed a lion with his bare hands as if it was a goat. He killed a thousand men with the jawbone of a donkey. The Holy Spirit's presence on his life enabled this kind of strength. But when he committed adultery, he was unaware the Holy Spirit had left him. The moment we lose the Holy Spirit is like letting the air out of a balloon. Don't grieve or quench the Holy Spirit—value that relationship above all and hold it dear. (Ephesians 4:29-31, 1 Thessalonians 5:19)

Psalm 51:12 – "Restore to me the joy of Your salvation and uphold me in Your generous Spirit."

God's generous Spirit will not only restore our joy but also help it to remain in us. Otherwise, we'll be happy one day and sorrowful the next. Christians will have trouble, no doubt, but it does not have to be everlasting. Psalm 30:5 says, "He will turn our mourning to dancing." Psalm 30:11 says, "Weeping will endure for a night, but joy will come in the morning." We can overcome.

Jesus Christ bore every sorrowful situation for us. Let's ask God with the help of the Holy Spirit to restore the joy of our salvation.

CHAPTER SEVENTEEN

Spirit of Life

The good influence of the Holy Spirit in our lives will give us the life God intended—the life of Jesus Christ, an abundant, resurrected, and long life. God Almighty wants to give us the Spirit of Life. Let us consider the blessing that we will receive when we are influenced by the Spirit of Life. The Apostle Paul said,

> *"For we who live are always delivered to death for Jesus' sake, that the life of Jesus may also be manifested in our mortal flesh. So then death is working in us, but life is in you. And since we have the same spirit of faith according to what is written, I believed and therefore I spoke. We also believe and therefore we speak." (2 Corinthians 4:11)*

When the life of Jesus Christ manifests in our mortal flesh, His life will reflect through our life upon the lives of the people.

Jesus spoke every word by faith and without doubt. We can speak the same way and overcome any negative thoughts or feelings. Have faith in Jesus Christ. His life will manifest in you through the Holy Spirit. Then we will be able to walk and talk like Jesus Christ.

Romans 8:1-2 holds a key:

> *"There is therefore now no condemnation for those who are in Christ Jesus, who do not walk according to the flesh, but according to the spirit. For the law of the Spirit of Life in Christ Jesus has made me free from the law of sin and death."*

When we are under the influence of the Spirit of Life, there is no condemnation when we believe Jesus. However, we should not walk according to the lust of the flesh or the works of the flesh. Only then will we have no condemnation. Many people avoid this part of the verse and say, "For one who is in Christ, there is no condemnation." God Almighty always wants there to be no condemnation in our lives if we avoid the work of the flesh. So the law of the Spirit of Life in Christ Jesus has made me free from the law of sin and death. We must live a free life as Christians, always liberated. (Galatians 5:1, 13)

That is why the Spirit of Life manifesting in our lives is very important. If we don't want any condemnation in our lives, we must walk in the freedom of holiness and avoid the works of the flesh, which are written in Galatians 5:19-20.

> "Now the works of the flesh are evident which are adultery, fornication, uncleanliness, lewdness, idolatry, sorcery, hatred, contention, jealousies, outbursts of wrath, selfish ambition, dissension, heresy, envy, murder, drunkenness, revelry and the like of which I tell you, just as I told you in time past, that those who practice such things will not inherit the kingdom of God."

So, we may be Christians, and we may do a lot of things. However, if we don't manifest the life of Jesus Christ with the influence of the Spirit of Life, we will not be able to bring others to the light of Jesus. For that, we must avoid the works of the flesh.

Before we know Jesus, we indulge in all of the lusts of the flesh. However, Jesus Christ delivered us from these dark deeds. God Almighty delivered us to the kingdom of Jesus. We must live like a king's child in that kingdom. (Colossians 1:13) We must determine that we don't want any of the works of the flesh so that the Spirit of Life will manifest in us.

Genesis 2:7 says, "The Lord God formed man from the dust of the ground and breathed into his nostrils the breath of Life." Man became a living soul. Here is the basic concept: only when the Spirit of Life manifests will we be able to do what Jesus Christ did on this earth. We will be able to live out what the Bible says. Because of

God's mercy, He treats us like children. He has pity on us because He knows our frame is of dust. (Psalm 103:13-14)

So when the Spirit of Life comes, what happens?

Our life will become a role model to others. When we leave this earth, our legacy will be as a role model for generations to come. When you see the lives of Elijah and Moses, the Bible says they were like you and I. (James 5:16-17; Exodus 2:12) Remember that Moses was a murderer, but God showed tremendous mercy. Because of mercy, He made these men's lives a blessing. (Romans 9:16) In Revelation 11:1-11, God is saying, "Take the measuring rod, measure the temple, measure the altar, and measure the people therein."

You must understand we are not structures. So why is God saying "measure the people therein"? God wants to measure not only the temple and the altar, but also our spiritual lives.

How are we measuring up in the sight of the Lord?

It is not enough to remain baby Christians lifelong. We must have the depth of the experience of God. Only when we have the influence of the Spirit of Life will the measurement be successful. God wants to measure our spiritual lives, but unless we are influenced by the Spirit of Life, we will not have the depth of intimate relationship that God wants when we are worshipping the Lord.

That is why God says that in the end times there will be many Gentiles that will rise up all around in order to crush Jerusalem. God said, "Don't measure the outer courts. The outer courts belong to the Gentiles." Jerusalem is surrounded by Gentile nations. As Christians, we are similarly surrounded by worldly influences all around us.

The world wants to crush us and tread upon us.

God says, "There are two olive tree branches which are the two witnesses, one who converted the water into blood; one who brought the fire from Heaven, who shut the heavens for three and a half years." (Revelation 11:3-4)

He is speaking of Moses and Elijah. God also tells us that the devil is loosed from the bottomless pit to rise up in a great measure. Then these two witnesses will come and, like mighty prophets, do great works. The devils and wicked people will tremble.

Finally, the antichrist will come and kill the two witnesses, and they will be seen lying in the streets of Jerusalem for three and a half days. The entire world will see and celebrate their death. The Gentiles will say, "No one can rule us." They will send gifts to one another to celebrate the good news that the two witnesses are dead.

Because of satellite television and the Internet, we now comprehend how it is possible for the Bible to say the entire world will see. But after three and a half days, God will raise them up by sending the Spirit of Life – the Spirit of Breath. "Now after three and a half days the breath of life from God entered them and they stood

on their feet. Great fear fell upon those that saw them."
(Revelation 11:11)

When the Spirit of Life enters our lives, the enemy
always fears us, but we need not fear the enemy. This is
how God takes us to the next level of spiritual growth.
We must decide to manifest the life of Jesus Christ that
God originally intended for our lives.

When the Spirit of Life enters us, what will happen?

"If you die with Christ, you also live with him." (Romans 6:8) In 1 Corinthians 15:45, the Bible says, "The
first man Adam became a living being." The last Adam,
Jesus Christ, became a life-giving Spirit. That is why we
must depend upon the last Adam to be able to enjoy His
life of abundance, resurrection and longevity. When the
Spirit continuously manifests upon our life, we will have
longevity of life and overcome sickness.

God will help us by the Spirit of Life. In Numbers 11,
when the spirit was upon Moses, God took that spirit and
put it upon seventy people. All seventy people started
prophesying. That is why Moses was able to say, "Like
unto me God raised among you a prophet." (Deuteronomy
18:15-18) That kind of reflection of the Spirit is in us.

Once upon a time, Moses was a murderer. Afterward,
he is reflecting the glory and presence of God. (Exodus
34:28-29, 35) "His face shone." The meaning of this is
found in Numbers 6:24-26. The Bible says, "May God

lift up the countenance of His presence upon you, may God shine His face upon you." This kind of reflection came upon Moses. God's anointing came as well. We see in Deuteronomy 34:7 that, at 120 years of age, his eyes did not dim. He was strong. He killed a man when he was forty, and then spent forty years in the desert. God made him a leader at eighty, and God was with him. You cannot become a mighty prophet unless you are led by the Spirit. (2 Peter 1:21) These holy men spoke when they were moved by the Holy Spirit.

May God Almighty give you this kind of reflection when you walk under the good influence of the Spirit of Life. God will give you life and longevity of life. (Psalm 91:15-16) "As you know His Name, He will hold you in high esteem and place you on the highest rock. God will satisfy you with long life. God will give you an abundant life." This means that what we were not able to achieve before, we will now be able to achieve under the abundance of God. Whatever trials we have undergone, God will see us through. Psalm 66:12 says, "God, you caused men to ride over our heads. We have gone through the fire and water, but at last, you brought us to the place of abundance." Though you may have undergone many difficult situations, when the Spirit of Life comes, God's abundance will start flowing.

That is why Jesus Christ is known as the Prince of Life. (Acts 3:15) That is why uneducated people like Peter, John and James transformed when God's Spirit of Life manifested upon them. (Acts 4:13) When Peter walked among people, even his shadow healed the sick. (Acts 5:15) John the Apostle received the revelation about the future things that we are seeing today. Two thousand years later, those same events are taking place—the events remembered in the Book of Remembrance because he received the revelation of Jesus Christ by the Holy Spirit. That is why it is known as the Book of Revelation, which is so accurate that God does not want us to alter anything written in it. (Revelation 1:1) God said anyone who alters what is written there will be subject to plagues and diseases. (Revelation 22:17-19)

God will give you the same kind of abundance Peter and John had. Even if you are educated, even if you have a degree, why don't you ask God to fill you more and more with the Spirit of Life? Allow God to manifest the life of Jesus upon you. That is why Jesus said, "As I live, you also live." (John 14:19) That is the abundant life that God wants us to live.

God is expecting us to allow Him to take us to deeper experiences. This is only possible when we obey the Spirit, instead of the lust of the flesh. When we die with Christ, we also live and reign with Him. This is what God intends for us the moment we obey. God wants us to be up above all the people of the nations. (Deuteronomy 28:1) God has already seated us in the heavens along with Christ because of His resurrection power. (Ephesians 2:6) The power, the Spirit of Glory, the Spirit of Resurrection, that same Spirit will come upon our lives in the same way it raised Jesus Christ from death to life. (Romans 8:11; Romans 6:4) We must get ready!

After we receive abundant life, we must walk in the resurrected life. When you are in a hopeless condition, you can be resurrected by the same spirit that raised Jesus, because God Almighty is a holy God who lives in the high places. When we are in broken or hopeless situations, He wants to restore us, raise us and cause us to sit with Jesus Christ. What blessed people we are!

We see in Ezekiel 37:1-14 that the hand of the Lord came upon Ezekiel and took him to the midst of a valley full of dry bones. God said, "Son of man, can these dry bones live?" Ezekiel didn't reply, "No, Lord, You must be joking." His reply was, "Oh Lord, You know." When God sends the Spirit of Life, even dead things will come back to life.

Verse 4 says, "Oh dry bones, hear the Word of the Lord." God asked him to prophesy. That is why what we believe and release from our mouths, God will cause even the dead things to come back to life because we are influenced by the Spirit of Life.

Verse 5 says, "Surely I will cause breath to enter into you, and you shall live." That is why even when we are in a dead or most hopeless condition, God wants to put the breath of Life, the Spirit of Life, in us.

God said in verse 6, "I put the breath in you, you shall live." When Jesus Christ rose from the dead on the third day and met the disciples, He breathed on the apostles and said, "Receive the Holy Spirit." (John 20:22) He intended not only for the disciples but for us as well to receive the resurrected life like He did.

In verse 10, Ezekiel prophesied, "Breath, come upon them." Those dry bones came to life and stood upon their feet as an exceedingly great army. In your life when the Spirit of the Breath of Life comes, you will be like a soldier for Jesus Christ. Let us not indulge or be entangled in the affairs of this world. (2 Timothy 2:4-10)

God said in verse 11, "Oh house of Israel, they indeed say, 'Our bones are dry, our hope is lost, we ourselves are cut off.'" The good news is that our hope shall never be cut off when we believe the God of hope. (Proverbs 23:18; Romans 15:13) That God of hope is the Lord Jesus Christ. Allow Him to send you the Holy Spirit because the very purpose for which Jesus Christ came to this earth was to baptize us with the Holy Spirit and with fire. (Matthew 3:11) In the same way that the Holy Spirit came upon Jesus so that, from that day, He walked with newness of life, may God Almighty do the same for us.

In Ezekiel 37:14, God said, "I will put my Spirit in you, and you shall live." Let us live a life like Jesus Christ. That is what God intends for our lives. Allow God to put His Spirit in you today.

Psalm 21:3-4 says, "Let God Almighty encounter you every day, give you the blessing of goodness, and crown you with pure gold."

When we ask for the Spirit of Life, He will give us abundant life. May God Almighty bless us as we walk under the influence of the Spirit of Life.

CHAPTER EIGHTEEN

From Glory to Glory

When we are under the good influence of the Spirit of Truth, the Holy Spirit will glorify God through us and take us from glory to glory. Many times we want to see our own reflection, but God wants His reflection to be seen in our lives. People under the influence of the Good Spirit will never glorify themselves or boast about themselves. Instead, the sign that they are under that influence is that they always want to glorify the name of God.

The Bible says in John 16:13-15,

"However when the Spirit of Truth has come, He will guide you in all truth for He will not speak on His own authority, but whatever He hears He will speak. He will tell you the things to come. He will glorify Me for He will take up what is mine and declare it to you.

*All things that the Father has are mine. Therefore I
said, 'He will take up mine and declare it to you.'"*

What a wonderful experience! Wherever we go, we
meet many people, Christians and Gentiles, who often want to speak about what they've accomplished. "I
achieved this much." " My church has this many members."
"I am this wealthy." There is no truth in such boasting.
The Truth alone is God Almighty.

God Almighty Jehovah is Truth. Jesus Christ is Truth.
The Holy Spirit is Truth. The absence of a lie is truth,
and the Truth is the Lord Jesus Christ Himself. (John 14:6)
We must overcome the lying spirit. (1 Kings 22:22) Jesus
Christ said, "From the beginning Satan is the father of
lies." (John 8:44) One lie breeds another lie. That is why
we must pray every day. "God give me the grace not to
speak a lie, that there would be no occasion to speak a
lie. Give me the grace to speak the truth, which is your
Word." (John 17:17) When we are influenced by the Spirit
of Truth, we will automatically glorify the name of Jesus
Christ. That is why we must pray, "Let us walk all the days
of our lives under the influence of the Spirit of Truth
who will guide us into all truth."

When we walk under the influence of the Spirit of
Truth, only then will He guide us because the Holy Spirit
will not speak under His own authority. Whatever He
hears, He will speak. Here you must understand when
the Lord Jesus Christ was sojourning on the earth for
thirty-three-and-a-half years, He lived three-and-a-half
years for ministry. He said, "What My Father does in

Heaven I see. What My Father speaks I hear, obey and judge according to that." (John 5:19; John 5:30)

This is why, when we are under the influence of the Spirit of Truth, the Holy Spirit will speak by the authority of Jesus, and not on His own authority. In Matthew 28:18-20 Jesus Christ said, "All authority under heaven and earth is given unto Me. Go and baptize people in the name of the Father, Son and Holy Spirit. Make them disciples, and lo I will be with you until the end of the age." God Almighty will give you the same authority that He gave to Jesus. You will be able to see Him practically exercising that authority through your life when you walk under the influence of the Spirit of Truth.

When you pray in the name of Jesus, the Holy Spirit alone will take your prayers to heaven. (Romans 8:26) And what Jesus is saying to the Father on your behalf as He intercedes for you, the Holy Spirit, will in turn, bring it back and declare it unto you. (Hebrews 7:25) That is why John 16:14 says, "He will glorify Me for He will take what is Mine and declare it to you."

We are all created to glorify Jesus Christ alone. We are not to glorify ourselves or any man. We are created for His Glory. (Isaiah 43:7) When we leave our sinful nature and confess our sins every day, automatically God's name will be glorified through us. (Joshua 7:19) As Christians under the good influence of the Spirit of Truth, we must do good work so that God's name will be glorified through us and our light will shine.

The brightness of the glory of God will be reflected in our lives. (Matthew 5:16) We will bear much fruit so the Father's name in Heaven will be glorified. (John 15:8) Then our body and spirit will glorify Almighty God. (1 Corinthians 6:19-20)

As a Christian, whenever we suffer, we need not feel ashamed. Instead, glorify the name of the Father. (1 Peter 4:16) We must ask God to fill us with the Holy Spirit of Truth. John 15:16 says, "All the Father has is mine." Whatever Father God kept belongs to Jesus, "Therefore I said that you will take of mine and declare it to you." Whatever you ask in the name of Jesus, what the Father kept, we are able to get only in the name of Jesus, and we access it through the Holy Spirit.

If we are declaring a testimony that we have made a profit in our business, that we have a good marriage, and so on , the way we can speak is to declare, "This is what the Heavenly Father has given or done for me."

The God of Glory appeared to our father Abraham in Acts 7:2. We are all blessed today under the same covenant that God gave Abraham. (Genesis 12:2-3; Hebrews 11:8-10)

Under the covenant of a thousand generations, how is it that we are blessed today?

In the same way Abraham, Isaac, Jacob and David were all blessed under that covenant—because of God's Glory that raised Jesus Christ from death to life (resurrected spirit); that same spirit will raise us up when we are filled with the Spirit of Truth. (Romans 6:4, Romans 8:11)

When that Spirit comes and reflects how the Spirit raised Jesus from death to life, the same Spirit of Glory will manifest upon our human flesh.

> *"But rejoice to the extent that you are a partaker of Christ's suffering that when His glory is revealed so you may also be glad with exceeding joy if you are approved for the name of Christ. Blessed are you for the Spirit of Glory and of God rests upon you." (I Peter 4:14)*

What a wonderful promise! Jesus Christ is the brightness of God's glory and the expressed image of His person. (Hebrews 1:3) When that same glory comes upon us, not only will we be delivered, but God will take us from glory to glory. (2 Corinthians 3:17-18)

Why are we losing the glory?

We are losing the glory because we are not under the influence of the Spirit of Truth. From time to time, when the devil is speaking lies, we are believing those lies. We are not believing the Truth of Almighty God. That is why I encourage you today to believe the Spirit of Truth. Be under that influence. Enjoy the glorious things that God has for you and He will take you from glory to glory.

CHAPTER NINETEEN

Spirit of the Fear of the Lord

When you are under the good influence of the Holy Spirit and the enemy comes in like a flood, God will raise up a standard against your enemies. Nowadays enemies are rising all around us. We don't know who we can trust, or who we shouldn't trust. We are not sure what is going to happen. Circumstances around us are becoming more and more uncertain. We may be doing good to others and yet, facing so many difficulties and even suffering. People are rising against us. People are trying to persecute us. God alone can help us by His Holy Spirit.

Isaiah 59:19 says, "So shall they fear the name of the Lord from the west and His glory from the rising of the sun. When the enemy comes in like a flood, the Spirit of the Lord will raise up a standard against him." When we are under the influence of the Holy Spirit, He will lift up a standard against Lucifer and against the demons.

What is God expecting? We must fear the name of the Lord.

If we want to fear God, we require the Spirit of the Fear of the Lord that was upon Jesus Christ. (Isaiah 11:2) Only when we decide to walk upright will we fear God. A righteous man fears God. (Genesis 42:18) I encourage you today to choose to walk in the fear of the Lord.

God's Glory is covering the entire earth because he is the God of Glory. He dwells in the marvelous light where no man is able to reach. (1 Timothy 6:16) From that position, He is looking and knows all of our afflictions. God will not only deliver us, He will lift up a standard against the devil, so he won't dare to touch us when we are under the influence of the Good Spirit when the enemy comes in like a flood.

When the flood comes, we often don't know where it originates from, even when the water is all around. But here is the good news, God said,

> *"Oh Jacob, you are my chosen one. Oh Israel, I made you. Even though you walk through the waters, it won't overflow you. Even though you walk through the fire, it won't burn you. Lo, I am with you." (Isaiah 43:2-3)*

The same God is with us. Not only that, but when we go through the fire and water, God will take us to a place of abundance. (Psalm 66:12)

That is why we must trust the power of the Holy Spirit. Jesus Christ said, "When the Holy Spirit comes upon you, you will get new power." (Acts 1:8) That is why, when the enemy comes in like a flood, the Spirit of the Lord will lift up a standard against him.

We must understand that Jesus Christ said, "The Spirit of the Lord is upon me." (Isaiah 61:1-2; Luke 4:18)

Why?

When the Spirit of the Lord was upon Jesus, He was able to proclaim the good news to the poor, sight to the blind, healing to the brokenhearted, healing to the wounds of the people, deliverance to the captives, and the year of the Lord's favor. The same Spirit, the Spirit of the Lord, is God Jehovah.

Now, in the New Testament, God wants to give the Spirit of His Son, Jesus Christ, so we can call the Heavenly Father our Abba Father. We will become sons and daughters. The spirit will witness to us, and we become heirs of God, and co-heirs with Jesus Christ. (Romans 8:14-16)

That is why I encourage every one of you today, whatever your situation, realize that there is an opportunity with the help of the Holy Spirit. We will be raised up and kept in the top position, not because of our greatness, but because of the Lord. Increase does not come from the east or the west, but from the Lord. (Psalm 75:6-7) Do not fear bad news. Trust in the Living God. (Psalm 112:7-8)

The time has come for you. When there is a flooding situation all around you, you may be suffering from problems. I bring you good news. God's promise says, "The afflictions of the righteous are many but God will deliver from them all." (Psalm 34:19) You may be having financial difficulties, you may have lack of spiritual insight, you might be crushed and broken in your heart, you may have a situation where you are captivated, or you may be waiting and hoping this year something good will happen; yet nothing is happening. But when the Spirit of the Lord comes, He will lift up a standard against the devil who came against you like a flood. In this season, God Almighty is going to bless you tremendously.

The Bible says in Psalm 145:14, "The Lord God Almighty upholds all who fall and raises up all who are bowed down; bowed down with toil, disease and poverty." The Lord opens the eyes of the blind. The Lord raises those who are bowed down. The Lord loves the righteous. (Psalm 146:8)

Are you bowed down?

This is the time through the Holy Spirit influence that you will be raised up. This is what God intends. In Exodus 19:4-6, God said, "I carried you on eagles wings. I brought you to Myself. Obey My voice. Keep My covenant. You will be a special treasure to Me above all the people for the earth is Mine. You will be kings and priests, a holy nation." It is wonderful that God Almighty will not only deliver us from the flood effect of the devil, but also lift up a standard against him; and no demonic spirit can overcome the Holy Spirit.

Everytime, Jesus Christ casts out the devil by His Word. (Matthew 8:16) He did this by walking under the influence of the Holy Spirit. Jesus said in Luke 11:20, "If I cast out demons by the finger of God, the kingdom of God has come." In the same way, He said in Matthew 12:28, "By the power of the Holy Spirit when I cast out the devils, the kingdom of God comes."

Child of God, whatever your current condition—bowed down, pressed in—the good news is that you can walk under the influence of the Spirit of the Lord and He will lift up a standard against the devil. From this day not only will God solve the problem and crush the devil, but He will also lift you up to be with Jesus Christ.

The Bible says in Deuteronomy 33:27, "He is your eternal God, your rock and refuge." His everlasting arm will be beneath you. He will stand before you and strike the enemy. God Almighty was with the children of Israel when they were walking into the Promised Land. They were led by a cloud by day and a pillar of fire by night. God traveled with them. Even when the Israelites were in bondage for four hundred years, God was with them. (Exodus 13:20, 21)

The same God will be with us. God Almighty stoops down to make us great. (Psalm 18:35) Will a rich man, a senator or a president come, stoop down and lift you up? Jesus Christ, who is God in Heaven, stooped down to become a man for you. (1 Timothy 3:16) You must trust the Lord Jesus Christ and His Spirit, the Spirit of the Lord which was upon Jesus. When the same Spirit that raised Jesus Christ from death to life is upon you, you will live under a different influence. (Romans 8:11; Romans 6:4) No more can the devil make you fall down. God Almighty by His Holy Spirit will raise you up from this season.

The Apostle Paul said in 2 Timothy 4:18, "God Almighty, Jesus Christ, rescues you from all evil and brings you to His Heavenly kingdom." Is it not wonderful? We must be under the Holy Spirit influence like a leaven in the Kingdom of Heaven. (Matthew 13:33) Then we will be able to overcome when the enemy comes in like a flood. God Almighty will lift up a standard against it. If we are trustworthy in small matters, God will make us great and make us rulers of many cities. (Luke 19:17) We can only trust what the Bible says if we have the influence of the Holy Spirit. Without the influence of the Holy Spirit, we will not be able to trust God.

God will lift us up to judge the enemy. No more will the enemy judge us. (1 Corinthians 6:2; 2 Corinthians 6:10) We are going to judge the poverty brought by the devil. The anointing upon us will make people rich. The enemy may be inflicting evil, but God Almighty will use us and lift us up.

We see in the Bible that Joseph, the eleventh child of Jacob, was hated by his brothers for his dreams. They threw him into a pit, but God Almighty lifted him up. Joseph received visions and dreams by the Holy Spirit anointing. (Genesis 37:1-11; Acts 2:17; Joel 2:28) Without the influence of the Holy Spirit, we can't dream what God intended for our future or what He has kept for us. The devil may put us down, but God is calling us as sons and daughters.

As we already discussed in Chapter 4, Joseph was overpowered in the natural realm, but the Spirit of God was with him. (Genesis 39:2-5; 41:38-42; 45:7-9) After Joseph was thrown into the pit, he was then sold as a slave to Potiphar's house. God was with him, and his owners saw it. Everything Joseph attempted was successful. Everything he touched was prosperous. God blessed the house of Potiphar for Joseph's sake.

Even though Joseph lived a holy life and did well for his master, remember that he was put in prison because of Potiphar's wife. Through her accusation, the mouth of the enemy testified, "This Hebrew boy whom you brought." (Genesis 39:9-14) People may try to accuse us, but the Spirit of the Lord is with us, as He was with Joseph. Jesus said, "I came to set the captives free." (Luke 4:18-19) Let the same Holy Spirit be with you and lift up a standard against the enemy. Even in prison, Joseph found favor in the sight of the guards. He was able to interpret the dreams of the baker and the cupbearer. Exactly according to the dreams, the cupbearer was restored to his position and once again stood before the king, even though he forgot Joseph. But when the king had a dream that no one could interpret, God put Joseph in the remembrance of the cupbearer.

Then Joseph was brought to Pharaoh where he was enabled by God to interpret the king's dream exactly and tell the meaning of what God was going to do. Pharaoh said in reference to Joseph, "Can we find this kind of spirit in any man?" Joseph had the Spirit of Wisdom, Knowledge, Understanding and Discernment. He became ruler of the entire nation under Pharaoh and became like a father to Pharaoh as ruler over his household and a prime minister to the nation.

Even though Joseph's brothers did him harm, what was his attitude? He said, "You meant evil in my life. You threw me into the pit to kill me, but God used it for good." We must develop this same attitude. Joseph was written about in the book of faith warriors. (Hebrews 11:22) At approximately 110 years of age, he gave instructions to the children of Israel regarding his bones before he died. He wanted to be buried in the Promised Land. Because his bones were taken by the children of Israel, God Almighty divided the Red Sea, divided the Jordan, made the walls of Jericho fall down, and God allowed the children of Israel to enter the Promised Land flowing with milk and honey, all because Joseph was under the influence of God.

The enemy came in like a flood—his brothers hated him and sold him as a slave, Potiphar's wife gave him trouble, and he was forgotten in prison. However, in the midst of every pressing situation, God lifted and elevated him. The same God will lift and elevate us.

The Lord sends both poverty and wealth. He humbles and exalts people. (1 Samuel 2:7; Psalm 75:7; Proverbs 22:1-2) Consider the life of Daniel in Daniel 2:21. He was a captive and then a slave. He was able to interpret the dream of the king even when the wise men, magicians and sorcerers could not. Daniel said, "God Almighty changes the times and the seasons. He sets up and disposes of kings. He gives wisdom to the wise and knowledge to the discerning." This kind of faith is how an ordinary slave boy, Daniel, became a prime minister. We serve such a great God!

An order was given to put Daniel into the den of lions because he was worshipping the God of Israel. (Daniel 6:10) Even though a decree was passed to worship the king, he opened the windows towards Israel and knelt down to pray three times a day like usual. The enemy came in like a flood, but Daniel never feared because he was under the influence of the Holy Spirit. God sent His angel and shut the mouths of the roaring lions. He protected and elevated Daniel. The enemy might bring scary situations like a flood, and you may be thinking there is no hope. Call upon God and cry, "I want the influence of the Spirit of the Lord upon me. The Spirit that influenced Jesus, Joseph, and Daniel, let that same Spirit come upon me."

When the same Spirit was upon David, God lifted him up. (1 Samuel 16:13) That is why he wrote, "He will raise up the poor and needy out of the dust and ashes and make them sit with the kings and princes." (Psalm 113:7-8) God made David, an ordinary shepherd boy, to be a king.

In the same way, God is calling you to be a king and a priest for him. (Revelation 1:6) That is why 2 Samuel 7:8 says, "Tell my servant David this is what the Lord Almighty says, 'I took you from the pastures and following the flock to make you ruler over the people of Israel.'" God will do the same for us. Just as God promoted unworthy men and women in the Bible, the same God will raise us up.

The people who know their God will do great exploits. That is why we must know the good influence of the Holy Spirit. The Spirit of the Lord is upon us. Even though the enemy comes in like a flood against us, God will lift up a standard against him. No flood or fire can burn or overtake us. God is with us! He wants to lift us up in the midst of difficult situations. Jesus Christ said, "With men this is impossible, but with God all things are possible." (Matthew 19:26-30) Jesus said, "He left everything for Me but where the Son sits on the throne of glory you will also sit on the thrones and you will be judging." We are seated in the Heavens along with Jesus Christ. (Ephesians 2:6) When the good Spirit comes, not only will He lift up a standard, but He will also lift us up.

CHAPTER TWENTY

Feed My Sheep

This chapter is for all the shepherds. Psalm 143:10 says, "Teach me to do your will, O Lord, You are my God. Lead unto the land of the plain. Give me your Good Spirit." Under the influence of the Good Spirit alone, we are able to walk in the land of the plain. Otherwise the devil, the crooked serpent, will create crooked ways. (Isaiah 45:1) Then we will have valleys, rugged paths, problem after problem, and we will become frustrated. But under the Spirit's influence, God Almighty will make us to walk in the plain and we will be like a leaven impacting the whole lump in the kingdom of God. (Matthew 13:33) Under the good influence of the Holy Spirit, we will become good pastors and overseers to work in the kingdom of God.

The Bible says in Acts 20:28, "Therefore take heed to yourself, unto all the flock which the Holy Spirit has given you to oversee and to shepherd the church of God, which He purchased with His own blood." Pastors, teachers, men of God, therefore take heed of the flock, which the Holy Spirit has made you overseers. The Holy Spirit alone called you into ministry to take care of the flock of God. That is why after the resurrection when Peter denied Jesus three times, He said to Peter, "Do you love me? Feed my sheep." This means take care of My flock. The same God is telling us to be a good shepherd like Jesus Christ.

The Holy Spirit has made us overseers. It is not because we have a Bible college degree or because someone offered us a job. If we have a real call on our lives and the understanding that we are called by the Holy Spirit, we must walk under the influence of the Holy Spirit; and not under our personal, sensual or earthly influence.

As shepherds of God, we are not our own. We were purchased for a price. Hence we must glorify God with our body and spirit. (1 Corinthians 6:19-20; 1 Peter 1:18) We are purchased by the blood of the Lamb. That is why as believers and servants of God we must always think, "We are not the boss. We are shepherds called by God." We see in Jeremiah 3:15 what God said about the pastors/shepherds: "I will give you shepherds according to My heart who will feed you with knowledge and understanding."

The shepherd must have the wisdom, knowledge, and understanding of God in order to lead the flock in the way they must walk all the days of their lives. For that purpose, we require the influence and help of the Holy Spirit.

Proverbs 27:23 says, "Be diligent to know the state of your flock." Shepherds of God must be diligent, and diligence comes only when we are under the good influence of the Holy Spirit. Whether our churches are big or small, it never matters. Fifty people or fifty thousand people never matters. God never said to different men, "You are a big pastor, and you are a small pastor." When we are faithful with fifty, God may give us five-hundred-thousand.

What is important, is our character, lifestyle and walk. When we walk under the Holy Spirit's guidance, people will be blessed through us. We can get this kind of wisdom, knowledge and understanding only when our trust is placed in Jesus Christ and we fear God. Wisdom is a spirit. Knowledge is a spirit. Understanding is a spirit. That is what Jesus Christ received. (Isaiah 11:2) That is why the Spirit of Wisdom came when Moses laid his hand on Joshua, and all the people began heeding Joshua the same way they heeded Moses. (Deuteronomy 34:9)

All wisdom, knowledge and understanding is hidden in Jesus Christ. (Colossians 2:3) This same Jesus Christ, will give us the same knowledge and understanding like a treasure in our lives when we fear Him because the Spirit of the Lord is upon us. (Isaiah 33:6) Man made pastors are often leading people to hell because they don't have the guidance or call of the Holy Spirit in their lives. It's important not to follow that kind of leader.

Those with the influence of the Holy Spirit automatically receive the Father's heart. That is why the Apostle Paul said, "You may have ten thousand teachers but you don't have many fathers. I begot you in the gospel of Jesus Christ. Therefore I urge you to imitate me." (1 Corinthians 4:15) This is why a pastor's life must be lived in such a way that it can be imitated by the body of Christ. Paul said, "Imitate me as I imitate Christ." (1 Corinthians 11:1) Let us not be man made pastors. Let us be led by the Spirit twenty-four hours a day and influenced by Him in our walk.

It is the Holy Spirit who makes someone an overseer. The Holy Spirit will give pastors understanding, knowledge and wisdom. Our understanding is the ability to know the truth of Jesus Christ. We must comprehend and interpret the meaning and purpose of our call from God through the Holy Spirit. Only then will we receive understanding. Ephesians 1:17-18 says,

"The God of our Lord Jesus Christ, the Father of Glory may give to you the Spirit of Wisdom and revelation in the knowledge of Him. The eyes of your understanding be enlightened that you may know what is the hope of His calling; what are the riches of the glory of His inheritance in the saints, and what is the exceeding greatness of His power toward those who believe."

This is the kind of wisdom, knowledge and understanding we must pray for. The God of our Lord Jesus Christ is Jehovah the Father of Glory. He will give us the Spirit of Wisdom and revelation in the knowledge of Him. Only when we get that revelation will we have the knowledge of Jesus Christ.

The moment we get the Spirit of Wisdom, people will heed what we have to say. We will also require mentors. Think of Moses and Joshua once again. We see in Joshua 11:15, "What God commanded Moses did. What Moses commanded Joshua did." In the same way, pastors require mentors who are walking in the Spirit, not in the flesh. When we have this kind of spiritual mentor and our lives are influenced by the Holy Spirit, we can automatically influence the congregation.

"The eyes of your understanding be enlightened." Only when our eyes are anointed by the Holy Spirit will we be able to see the true state of our lives. (Revelation 3:18) Otherwise, we may not be able to determine whether or not what we are doing is pleasing to God. God Almighty directed and counseled the people by the movement of His eye. (Psalm 32:8) God will give us the same kind of grace. Let us not be under a sensual, earthly or devilish influence. Let us not follow the things of the earth. We must follow what God says so that our eyes of understanding will be enlightened, that we may know what is the hope of His calling.

The fivefold ministry is a call from God, not from man, and we must be steadfast in the call. (Ephesians 4:1, 11) The pastor/shepherd is one of those five callings, and we must realize the hope of that call. Unless we know the God of Hope and trust Him in the midst of our trials and tribulations, we will not be able to understand—and that understanding requires Holy Spirit influence. The God of Hope is Jesus Christ. Whenever we suffer tribulation as men of God, we must wait patiently. When we do that, God gives the examination. When we pass the examination, God gives hope. That hope will never put us to shame. (Romans 5:2-5)

God Almighty alone can give understanding and enlightenment so that we will know the hope of our calling. As long as we look unto fleshly things—like who is or is not rich or giving a tithe, or inviting famous people into the church in order to draw a crowd—we will not be able to see the real plan and purpose of God. The church must be open. Rich or poor, everyone is equal in the body of Christ. It is only under the influence of the Holy Spirit that we will be able to understand the riches of glory of the inheritance of the saints. Jeremiah 17:5-6 says, "Cursed is the one who trusts in the flesh." God said, "He is like a thorny bush in the desert; even though good things are around him, he cannot see." What God purposed for us, we are not able to see when we depend upon people rather than upon the Holy Spirit.

When we know the hope of our calling, what happens?

Jeremiah 17:7-8 says, "We will become like a tree planted by the river brook of water; our leaves will be green even in the hot sun, and we won't stop bearing fruit in the drought." God Almighty who made us to be shepherds and called us by His spirit wants us to yield to the Spirit of Glory. Only then can we see the riches of the inheritance that He has kept for us and what is the exceeding greatness of His power toward those of us who believe according to His mighty works.

God wants to make us great pastors, but we must seek wisdom from Heaven as we are led by the Holy Spirit. Only then, will God be able to bless us. James 3:17 says, "The wisdom from Heaven is pure wisdom." We must have this wisdom in order to live a pure life. Wisdom from Heaven is peaceful— so we must be at peace with everyone. Wisdom from Heaven is meek—so we must not walk in pride or arrogance. Wisdom is yielding, so we must yield.

As pastors we want the people to yield, but we must also yield to the Holy Spirit. Like a grain of wheat, when we die to our sin and self, God will exalt our life as a pastor. Paul said, "I die daily." (1 Corinthians 15:31, Galatians 2:20) He said, "No more I live, but Jesus Christ lives in me." This is how God wants us to live. We must seek this kind of wisdom from God and be willing to yield. Merciful wisdom from Heaven bears good fruit. We must be filled with wisdom that has no hypocrisy to feed our flock. Only then will we make a good mark as a pastor. "Grace and peace be multiplied with you through the knowledge of God." (2 Peter 1:2-3)

As a pastor, when we have that knowledge of God's grace, peace will be multiplied in our church. We will see when our people depend upon grace, that grace is multiplied and people in our churches will become rich. Because of the anointing upon us, weak believers will be strengthened. (2 Corinthians 12:9) Under that multiplied grace, we will be able to build God's kingdom. The mountain of obstruction will be removed. All the people around us will say, "Grace, grace, grace unto it." (Zechariah 4:6-9)

The seven eyes are the seven spirits. Let God Almighty give you that kind of grace because Jesus Christ came to this earth for that purpose. Moses brought the law, but Jesus Christ brought grace and truth. He wants to give you grace after grace. Whatever your condition may be, until this time as a shepherd you may have walked under your own power, with your own biblical knowledge, with your computer, internet, YouTube, etc. I encourage you to leave these things behind and depend upon God's grace, not upon any man. When you do, God's grace and peace will be multiplied unto you. "Grace and peace be multiplied unto you; through the knowledge of God." (2 Peter 1:2-3) Life and godliness through the knowledge of Jesus has called us to glory and virtue. As shepherds, God Almighty wants us to have the knowledge of God and of our Lord Jesus Christ.

As the servants of God we should not imitate the world. We should not bring the world to the church. Rather, through our influence, the world must imitate the church. It is good for the boat to be in the water, but not good for water to be in the boat. In the same way, it is good when we are in the world so that we can lead people to salvation, but it is not good when the world is in us.

That is why as shepherds, we must be led by the Holy Spirit. Let God give us a glorious ministry with good values and virtue. As wise pastors, we will have increased learning, become men of understanding and give wise counsel to the church. Under the influence of the Holy Spirit, our negative traits will go away—like discontentment, impatience, wicked thoughts, mistrust, suspicion, pride and arrogance—and the fruit of the Holy Spirit will lead us.

We must never treat the flock of God with doubt or contempt. We must treat them with love because, as shepherds, we must feed the flock with wisdom, knowledge and understanding. If we are impressed with the world's systems, we will want to bring the world's system into the church. The church will then have a sensual influence instead of the influence of the Holy Spirit. When we are under the influence of the Holy Spirit, grace, joy, love and peace will multiply in our lives and in our churches.

CHAPTER TWENTY-ONE

Spirit of Truth

When the Spirit influences our lives, we will be able to influence God's Kingdom. (Matthew 13:33-34) The Good Spirit will help us to live a life of honesty and integrity before God and men. We see in Acts 6:3-5, during the time of the apostles, they were mainly concentrating on preaching the word, fasting, praying and breaking bread.

During those days, feeding the widows, children and poor people was becoming a burden to the apostles, so they came together and said, "From among you choose seven people who are full of the Holy Spirit, have the wisdom of God, and who are honest." When they said this, it pleased all of the people who heard the conversation. They appointed Stephen, Philip and others. Here is what we must understand.

Pertaining to any of God's kingdom work, whether we are a believer, pastor, apostle, teacher, prophet, or evangelist, God wants our lives to be full of the Holy Spirit. This means our lives must be led by the Spirit of God. Before we can become servants of God, we must be sons of God. Only when the Spirit leads us will we be known as the sons of God. Then when the spirit witnesses, we will be qualified to be heirs with God, co-heirs with Jesus Christ. (Romans 8:14) The apostles declared that anyone chosen must be filled with the Holy Spirit, but it is not only about gifts. A person must be full of the Holy Spirit—full of the fruit of the Spirit. (Galatians 5:22-23)

Only when we continually have the fruit of the Spirit will the Holy Spirit abide in us. Gifts and callings are irrevocable. (Romans 11:29) Even if we make many mistakes, we will still be able to speak in tongues or pray for healing. It is very important to understand that it is only when we are led by the Spirit that we will be able to lead effectively.

Next, the apostles said they were looking for those full of wisdom. Wisdom is not from man, but from God. Jesus Christ is that Wisdom. (1 Corinthians 1:24, 30-31) All wisdom, knowledge, and understanding are hidden in Christ Jesus. (Colossians 2:3) God wants to give us this level of wisdom. We will receive it when we ask. (James 1:5-6; James 3:17) When we get this wisdom, we are already qualified to serve Almighty God.

Third, the apostles were looking for honest men, those who had an honest report before men and God.

(2 Corinthians 4:11; 2 Corinthians 5:2) Paul says, "I have a pure conscience before men and God." When we have this type of honesty, our house and ministry will flow with abundant blessing. (Proverbs 28:20) Seeing that honesty, God will be faithful over our house. (Hebrews 3:3-5) God Almighty wants to bless us. As an example, let us look at two of the seven chosen by the apostles.

The first was Stephen. He was talking about how God brought the children of Israel from bondage and how they suffered and spent forty years in the wilderness because of their own rebellion and stubborn hearts. Stephen said, "Even today you have the same kind of stubbornness." When he spoke those words, they were very angry with him; in fact, they hit him and finally killed him with stones. As they were killing him, he said, "Father, don't put this sin upon them." Gazing heavenward, he said, "I see the glory of God on His throne and the Son of God standing on the right side."

. When they were throwing stones, he was not seeing those stones or hearing their abusive language. He was looking unto the Glory of God. (Acts 7:55-58)

What happened?

The people saw the face of Stephen and said he looked like an angel. (Acts 6:15) This is how God makes an exchange. We may suffer at times when we are living for God, but Jesus said, "In this world you will have tribulation, but be of good cheer for I have overcome the world. You also will overcome. I give my peace to you." That is why I encourage you, like Stephen, fix your eyes toward Heaven and the glory of God. Let us not focus on earth but rather look unto the Author and Finisher of our faith, Jesus Christ. (Hebrews 12:2)

Next, we see a man named Philip. When persecution rose up in Jerusalem, he did not run away or shut his doors and sit in one place praying. (Acts 8:1-8) Instead, he went to Samaria to proclaim the Gospel. He said, "The harvest is plentiful and ripe." When Jesus went to Samaria, the people believed. When the Samaritan woman went, they believed. But believing is not enough. A revival must begin.

Philip went to Samaria and proclaimed Jesus Christ as Lord and Savior. God did wonders, signs and miracles. The lame walked, the blind received sight, devils screamed and departed, and people were astonished. In the entire land of Samaria, there was joy. When we want to walk in this level of anointing and honesty, the Holy Spirit will dwell with us and in us. That makes the difference. It is the call of the Spirit of Truth, which will lead us unto all truth. The world cannot see or know the Spirit of Truth. (John 14:17)

We must pray daily to overcome the spirit of lies and walk in the truth of God. (1 Kings 22:22) The spirit of lies is the devil. Let us overcome and walk in the truth and integrity of God. Jesus said, "The devil is a liar and the father of lies from the beginning." (John 8:44) Therefore we must avoid lies and seek the help of the Holy Spirit, the Spirit of Truth. By the grace of the Lord, we can overcome the lying spirit and be honest before God and before people.

We see two people, Ananias and Sapphira, in Acts 5:1-10 who had property and told the apostles they would sell it and give all the money to the church. However, when they sold the property, they gave only a portion of what they received. Peter looked at Ananias and said, "Why has Satan filled your heart so you would speak a lie? You have not sold the property for this amount." The moment Ananias heard this, he fell down dead. Afterwards his wife came and told the same lie, to which Peter responded, "You did not lie to man, you lied to God." Then she died. Whatever we commit to do before God, we must keep those vows.

We must tell the truth before man. No one compelled Ananias and Sapphira to give all of the money. It was their choice. However, once they committed the money to the church, they became dishonest when they held it back. Because Peter was filled with the Holy Spirit and was able to discern their dishonesty, this filling of the Holy Spirit gave Peter courage. Earlier, we see in Matthew 26:56, 68-74 that Peter denied he knew Jesus and ran away, but the Holy Spirit later gave him boldness. (Acts 2:1-4)

God Almighty will bless all of us when we stir up the Holy Spirit. We must pray that more of the Spirit of Truth would dwell in us and ask for more of the Spirit of Light. We must pray for all the darkness to depart from us, that all of our words will be truthful words. We must pray that God Almighty will establish our words and perform the truthful counsel that we give to people. (Isaiah 44:26) Let us pray every day, "God give me the grace to be an honest and faithful man, to walk in integrity and serve You."

CHAPTER TWENTY-TWO

Filled with the Anointing

The Holy Spirit's desire is to speak with us early in the morning. We have to develop our ability to listen to Him. Many times we listen to people and become distracted by their voices, rendering us unable to hear the voice of the Holy Spirit.

When our desire is to hear the Holy Spirit, we must depend upon grace. When God Almighty is ready to speak, we must be ready to listen. We must pray, "God, speak to me the words of Your grace. I don't want to depend upon my own strength." We will hear only when the Holy Spirit comes upon us.

Jesus Christ said in Luke 4:18-19, 21-22,

"The Spirit of the Lord is upon me to preach the gospel to the poor, to heal the brokenhearted, to proclaim deliverance to the captives and recovery of sight to the blind, to set at liberty those who are oppressed, to proclaim the year of the Lord's favor."

Because the Spirit was upon Him, He said, "Today this Scripture is fulfilled in your hearing." The people were astounded by the words of grace that He spoke.

What is this "grace"?

Whatever situation we are going through, Jesus wants to speak the exact opposite. He wants the poor to become rich and the brokenhearted to be whole. He wants to open the eyes of those who are blind and show them God's vision. The "year of the Lord's favor" means we are not living in a disadvantaged position, but in a position of advantage with God. That is possible only when the Spirit reigns in us. Jesus said this Scripture is fulfilled in our hearing, so when we hear, only then will it be fulfilled. That is the word of His grace.

King David said, "God, cause me to hear the word of Your grace." Early in the morning, God is ready to speak; we must be attentive to hear His voice. Psalm 63:1-2 says, "O God, You are my God; early will I seek You; my soul thirsts for You, my flesh faints for You. In a dry and thirsty land with no water I have seen You in the sanctuary. I see Your power and Your glory."

It makes a difference in our lives when we seek Him early in the morning. At that time of day, we are not yet seeking our own plans. God has made it so that the closer we come, the better we will hear Him. This is only possible when we connect our spirit with His Spirit.

John the Apostle said in Revelation 1:10, "I was in the Spirit on the Lord's Day, and I heard behind me a great voice like a trumpet." We will hear His voice only when our spirit joins with God's Spirit in the early morning, when we are fresh and not yet busy with the things of the day. That is the time when it is very easy to connect our spirit with the Lord's Spirit. When we connect with the Lord's Spirit, we develop the ability to listen.

The Bible says in 1 Corinthians 6:17, "He who is joined to the Lord becomes one spirit with Him." Our human spirit is always there because that is how we were created at birth. When we are born again, the Holy Spirit joins with our spirit. However, many times our spirit is disconnected from the Holy Spirit. Think of how a cell phone sometimes fails to get reception; we don't have a proper signal, so we can't hear well or may get disconnected. In the same way, our human spirit can be disconnected from the Holy Spirit.

So how can we join our spirit back with the Lord's Spirit?

We should not grieve the Holy Spirit. Make a Holy Spirit checklist from Ephesians 4:29-32 and meditate on it for a season.

What are you doing that grieves the Holy Spirit? Confess anything you are struggling with, and God will help you.

Ephesians 4:29-32 says,

> *"Let no unwholesome word proceed out of your mouth, but only that which is good for building up, that it may give grace to the listeners. And do not grieve the Holy Spirit of God, in whom you are sealed for the day of redemption. Let all bitterness, wrath, anger, outbursts, and blasphemies, with all malice, be taken away from you. And be kind one to another, tenderhearted, forgiving one another, just as God in Christ also forgave you."*

The Holy Spirit must hover over our human spirit to bring life, and if not, we will become rotten as the years go by. "Corrupt" in the Greek is the same meaning as rotten fruit. When we were first saved, we had such excitement about going to church and sharing what happened to us; but as the years pass, it can become routine. If we are not linking our spirit constantly with the Holy Spirit, our excitement about the things of God will fade.

The Scripture mentions "bitterness." Bitterness grows in our lives when we do not forgive people. When we are wronged and allow bitterness to take root and grow in our hearts, that bitterness corrupts what God has in store for us. Bitterness separates us from grace. We have to pull out bitterness by the root; only then can grace come. Otherwise, we will despise grace.

Hebrews 12:15 tells us, "Watch diligently so that no one falls short of the grace of God, lest any root of bitterness spring up to cause trouble, and many become defiled by it." God is not taking away the grace; we are losing it ourselves when we allow wrong thoughts about someone else. That is why God says it is okay to be angry, but don't sin. We are human beings, but we can master everything with God's grace.

How were our forefathers able to hear the voice of the Lord? Let's look at the faith warriors:

Acts 7:2 says, "The God of Glory appeared to Abraham." The same glory is available to us in the New Testament by acknowledging that the birth, death and resurrection of Jesus Christ has taken place by the Spirit of Glory.

Romans 6:4 says, "Therefore we were buried with Him by baptism into death, that just as Christ was raised up from the dead by the glory of the Father, even so we also should walk in newness of life."

Romans 6:14 says, "For sin shall not have dominion over you, for you are not under the law, but under grace."

When we ask the Spirit of Glory to link with our spirit, He will appear and speak to us just as He did with Abraham. He will never allow sin to have dominion over us. Because we dwell in a sinful world, our eyes may unintentionally behold some filthiness by mistake. We may turn on the television and see something bad, but it doesn't have to have dominion over us. We can turn away if we seek the Spirit of Glory to manifest upon our flesh.

1 Peter 4:14 says, "If you are reproached because of the name of Christ, you are blessed, because the Spirit of Glory and of God rests upon you." A New Testament privilege for believers is that the Spirit of Glory can rest upon us if we ask. Take time to pray and say, "God, anything I do must bring glory to You. I want to listen to You. I want the Spirit of Glory to rest on me."

Genesis 12:1-3 declares, "Now the Lord said to Abram, Go from your country, your family, and your father's house to the land that I will show you. I will make of you a great nation; I will bless you and make your name great, so that you will be a blessing. I will bless those who bless you and curse those who curse you, and through you all families of the earth will be blessed."

God gave Abraham a condition for the blessing he offered; Abraham had to leave his father's house, all his kinsmen and start his journey. When God blesses us, we will become great people and a great nation. When He makes our name great, we will in turn become a blessing to others. That covenant is still active today.

Why?

"And the Scripture, foreseeing that God would justify the Gentiles by faith, preached the gospel in advance to Abraham, saying, 'In you shall all the nations be blessed.' Christ has redeemed us from the curse of the law by being made a curse for us – as it is written, 'Cursed is anyone who hangs on a tree.' So that the blessing of Abraham might come on the Gentiles through

Jesus Christ, that we might receive the promise of the
Spirit through faith. Now the promises were made to
Abraham and his Seed. If you are Christ's, then you are
Abraham's seed, and heirs according to the promise."
(Galatians 3:8, 13-14; 16:29)

God does not say, "and to seeds," meaning many, but "and to your seed," meaning one, who is Christ.

God preached the first gospel in Genesis 12:2-3. From that time until now, that first gospel and the words of His grace can be heard and enjoyed by us. The Spirit of Glory appeared and spoke. We are entitled to that same blessed life when we connect with the same Spirit of Glory.

The Spirit was disconnected from Abraham because he was told to leave his kinsmen and bring immediate family only, but he brought Lot. He entered the Promised Land not knowing where he was going. First, he encountered the famine. Second, his wife was taken captive, but God intervened and delivered her. The king had given lots of cattle and sheep for Sarah's sake. When the problem came, the king said, "What I have given you, I don't want back." The flock started multiplying, and Lot was with him. God still never spoke. There was fighting between Lot and Abraham's herdsmen. Abraham realized God was not with him and thought, "His blessing is here and I am carrying on, but I am not able to hear the voice of the Lord." When he talked to Lot about separating their flocks and going their separate ways, he said, "We are brothers." He allowed Lot to choose which land he would take, and Lot took all of the valuable land. He left Abraham in the position where he was when God called him.

This is the key in Genesis 13:14. "After Lot had departed from him, the Lord said to Abraham, 'Lift up now your eyes, and look from the place where you are, northward and southward and eastward and westward.'" Lot was with Abraham for ten years, and God was silent and never spoke the entire time. Once Abraham and Lot separated, God began to speak.

We must listen when God tells us to separate from any unwanted people or unwanted elements in our lives. At times, we are not willing to obey because we think we might hurt people. We stop listening to the voice of the Lord. Abraham thought, "He is my brother's son. He doesn't have a father. Why should I not take care of him?" He brought Lot along with good intentions, but nothing good came of it.

After Lot and Abraham separated, Lot was taken captive by a king and Abraham rescued him. (Genesis 14:11-16) In Genesis 19, Lot was living in Sodom and Gomorrah when the Lord was going to destroy the city. Abraham interceded for Lot, so God sent angels to get Lot and his family out of the city. Lot was delivered, but a cursed generation came through him and his daughters, called the Moabites and Ammonites. Nothing good came out of even this act of sympathy that Abraham performed for Lot. When we don't obey, we are simply cutting ourselves off from hearing the voice of the Lord.

We are to love everyone; there is no problem with that. But we need not have fellowship with the people God has not ordained for our lives.

Hebrews 7:6-8 says, "But this man, whose descent is not numbered among them, received tithes from Abraham and blessed him who had the promises. Without question, the inferior is blessed by the superior. In the one case mortal men receive tithes, but in the other he of whom it is witnessed that he is alive receives them." The promise will be converted into a blessing when we hear God and obey what He says. The lesser is blessed by the better.

We must always be mindful of listening to the Spirit or whether the Spirit is witnessing to our spirit. Romans 8:14-17 says,

> *"For as many as are led by the Spirit of God, these are the sons of God. For you have not received the spirit of slavery again to fear. But you have received the Spirit of adoption, by whom we cry, 'Abba, Father.' The Spirit Himself bears witness with our spirits that we are the children of God, and if children, then heirs; heirs of God and joint-heirs with Christ, if indeed we suffer with Him, that we may also be glorified with Him."*

The Spirit witnesses to our human spirit that we are children of God. That witnessing is so important. The father/child relationship can be built only when the Spirit witnesses to our spirit. When it is not, we can pray as usual, and we may receive certain things, or we may not.

Let us pray daily, "I don't want to depend upon my strength or ability. This day, I want to hear the word of Your grace. I want to depend totally upon You, God. Whatever You want me to do for my family, ministry, business, or myself, I will do anything You say."

CHAPTER TWENTY-THREE

Anointing Ourselves Through Prayer

Praying a certain way every day for the next year can transform your life. When you sit in His presence, the Holy Spirit will envelop and control you, and you will walk in the Spirit. When we are led by the Spirit, we are sons and daughters of God. We have the Spirit of adoption as sons/daughters and call God our Abba Father. We are heirs with God and co-heirs with Jesus Christ. (Romans 8:14-16)

First, before you pray, ask yourself whether you have grieved and quenched the Holy Spirit by anything found in Ephesians 4:29-31. Ask yourself whether you are guilty of any type of anger, wrath, bitterness, clamor, envy, murder or jealousy. Then pray this prayer to keep these things from taking root in your life:

God, I do not want to quench or grieve the Holy Spirit. This area is my drawback and this is what I'm struggling with. (List your sins specifically.)

I ask You to forgive me because Jesus Christ died for me on the cross, rose from the dead on the third day, and because of You, I am baptized by the Holy Spirit. Holy Spirit, I welcome You back.

Holy Spirit, come upon my head; dwell in me the same way You dwelled in Jesus. (Isaiah 61:1-3; Luke 4:18-19) I want to proclaim the good news to the poor and build their lives. (Paul said in 2 Corinthians 6:10 that even if it looks like we lack everything, we have made many rich.) God, enable me to release good words through my mouth so I can make the poor become rich; for that purpose, I need Your anointing on my head.

Help me to open the eyes of the blind. God, most people have natural sight, but they are not able to see Your Glory because the god of this age has blinded the eyes of the people. (2 Corinthians 4:4) That is why I ask You to open my mind so that I can understand in order to open the eyes of people. (Ephesians 1:17-18) I want to see this happen the same way You opened Hagar's eyes in Genesis 21:14-20, the way You opened Elisha's servant's eyes in 2 Kings 6:16-17. In this same way, Lord, anoint me so that I, under that anointing, am able to proclaim sight to the blind so unbelievers will believe.

God, I need Your anointing to heal broken hearts as You have healed my broken heart. There are so many peo-

ple around me with broken hearts. Like You, Jesus, I want to see the broken hearts healed as in Psalm 147:3 and Isaiah 57:15. You are the God that lifts up the brokenhearted. Jesus, anoint me with Your Holy Spirit for that purpose.

You said, when the Holy Spirit was upon You, You were able to set the captives free. Let the same Holy Spirit be upon me. Let my captivity turn away. When Job said, "I can do all things through Christ who strengthens me," You turned away his captivity. (Job 42:2-4) Give me the anointing for that purpose.

Allow me to proclaim the year of the Lord's favor. Wherever I go, let my life be favor to others and in the same way let me have favor for people. When You lived on this earth, You got favor before men and God. (Luke 2:52) As I am righteous by the Blood of the Lamb, bless me with favor like a shield. (Psalm 5:12) I want You to rule over me and place Your Spirit upon my spirit.

Holy Spirit, fill my brain that I may have the mind of Christ as in Galatians 3:1-2. Holy Spirit, anoint my mind and let me think like Jesus. Like Jesus, let my thoughts be higher thoughts. (Isaiah 55:8-9) I need Your anointing so that my mind will be on the things of Heaven, not bound by satanic influences.

Holy Spirit, anoint my face. Just as Moses' face was radiant after going to Mt. Sinai, in the same way, anoint me. (Exodus 34:28-29, 35) You said that You will bless and keep me, that You will cause Your face to shine upon me. (Numbers 6:24-26) That is the blessing You gave to the *children of Israel. In the same way, let Your anointing come upon me. Let Your face shine upon me, and Your countenance be lifted upon my face. For that purpose, I need Your anointing. When people look at my face, let them see Your face, God. In the same way, when I see others, let me see Your face in them. Let there be no hatred in me towards anyone. Jacob feared Esau, but when Esau saw his face, he said, "I see the face of God." (Genesis 33:10) You created everyone in Your image. (Genesis 1:2-27) For that purpose, anoint my face with radiance and let me look to the people's faces with the same radiance.*

Anoint my eyes. Let my eyes glow like Your eyes. Jesus, Your eyes are full of compassion, and You look on people with compassion. (Matthew 14:14) Holy Spirit, anoint my eyes to be filled with Your compassion towards people.

Anoint my lips. You know any unclean words that have come from my lips. Keep watch over my mouth as in Psalm 141:3. Sanctify my lips as in Isaiah 6:3-5. Holy Spirit, anoint my tongue and mouth; let there be no double talk or double mindedness through my tongue. Let my words be true. God, give me the anointing to speak Your very oracle without measure. (John 3:34; 1 Peter 4:11)

Anoint my nose and nostrils. When You breathed into Adam, Your breath made him a living being. O Lord, let Your life flow through me; let no deadly things live in me. (Genesis 2:7) For that purpose, breathe Your Holy Ghost into me. Jesus breathed on the disciples and said, "Receive the Holy Spirit." They received the Holy

*Spirit, and their life began transforming. (John 20:22)
In the same way, Lord, please kindly do this for me.*

*Anoint my throat so that it will be melodious
and sweet to You and to other people. (Song of Solomon 2:14) I'm like your dove flying in your cleft.*

Anoint my neck. I don't want to carry unwanted yokes in my life. May every yoke be broken on my neck today as in Isaiah 10:27.

*Anoint my shoulders. Jesus, the government of God
is upon your shoulders. (Isaiah 9:6-7) In the same
way, may the government of God be upon my shoulders so I can be a fellow laborer in that purpose.*

*Anoint my hands. You said, "Blessed is the one who
gives rather than receives." Let my hands be giving hands
all the days of my life as in Acts 20:35. Let my hands
become comforting hands. Just as You have comforted
me, let me comfort others. (2 Corinthians 1:4) Let my
hands be praying hands. When Moses lifted his hands,
there was a victory. (Exodus 17:11-15) Let my hands be
blessing hands. In Luke 24:50, You lifted Your hands and
blessed the people. Let my hands be healing hands. When
You laid Your hand, every single person was healed.
(Luke 4:40-41) In the same way, anoint my hands so
that wherever I lay my hands with faith in Jesus, let the
people recover from their sickness as in Mark 16:17-18.*

*Anoint my chest. You said You would give me the
breastplate of righteousness. Let me be able to turn many*

people towards Your righteousness and let me shine like the stars in the heavens. (Ephesians 6:12-16; Daniel 12:3)

Anoint my heart. You said, "Blessed are the pure in heart for they shall see God." (Matthew 5:8) I ask for purity of conscience in my heart. (2 Timothy 1:3-5) Sanctify my heart with your blood. (Hebrews 9:14) Create a new heart in me, and put a new spirit in me. Lord, let my heart think like Yours. Let my heart see new visions and dreams.

Anoint all my inward parts. Anoint my kidney, liver, gallbladder—every system that I can't see, just as You created me. (Psalm 139:13) When You anoint, everything will function normally so I will have physical and spiritual health. It's Your will that I live a whole and healthy life. You call health and healing to return back, flowing through Your Holy Spirit anointing as in Jeremiah 33:6.

Anoint my stomach and belly. Holy Spirit, fill me so living waters flow; bring the dead things back to life. (John 7:37-38; Ezekiel 47:12)

Anoint my back. So I can carry my burden and the burdens of others, I lay my burdens at Your feet. Give me Your rest, Lord, by Your holy presence as in Ezekiel 33:14 and Matthew 11:28.

Anoint my waist. You said, "Gird your loins with the belt of Truth." (Ephesians 6:12-16) With that weapon let me stand always for Your Truth. Holy Spirit and Spirit of Truth, come within me. Convict me if there is any sin in me. Convict me in what way I am righteous. Convict me of what is the next step I should

*take. Spirit of Truth, greet me, Lord, so that I can al-
ways glorify the name of Jesus. (John 16:8, 13-14)*

*Anoint my knees. Anoint me with the same grace as
Daniel, as he regularly knelt down and prayed before
You, and he never feared any persecution, even in the
lion's den. (Daniel 6:10-11) At Your Name every knee
shall bow down and every tongue will confess that You
are Lord. Each day let me kneel down in Your Presence
and surrender my life to You. (Philippians 2:9-11)*

*Anoint my feet. As You anointed the feet of Abraham,
You said, "Wherever you walk to the north, south, east
or west, where you tread, I will give you those places for
you and your generations. (Genesis 13:14-16) You said to
Joshua, "Wherever you go and stand, I will give those
places to you and no one will be able to stand against
you." (Joshua 1:3-9) In the same way, God, anoint my feet
so that wherever I go in Your name I carry Your blessing.*

*Anoint my soul. God, Jehovah, You made Adam a liv-
ing soul. (Ezekiel 37:14; Genesis 2:7) In the same way, let
the living life flow in me by the Holy Spirit, and let my
soul become a living soul always praising You, Lord— not
grumbling, instead, always remembering Your goodness.
Let bad things not happen anymore. (Psalm 103:1-2)*

*Anoint my human spirit. The human spirit is the lamp
of God, but without oil the lap cannot glow. Holy Spirit,
come join with my human spirit and let me become one
spirit with You so that I can glorify You, by my body and*

by my spirit. (1 Corinthians 6:17, 19-20) God, I belong to You, so anoint every part of my body from head to toe.

AMEN

Make a list of everything that you think is holding you down and all of the things that you fear. Give names to all of those flaws and so-called character defects, those tiny imps on your shoulder that whisper in your ear and keep you up at night. For each demon, ask God, "What is the opposite of this thing? What would You like me to do? How would You like me to be?" Write them down, and then tear up the first list. You won't need it anymore. Live from your second list, the list of positives that you took from all that negative—the list that the angel on your shoulder sang to you—and smile.

Count it all joy, and smile.

MEET THE AUTHOR
DAVID TURNER

David Turner is an international businessman and healing evangelist, traveling the world at his own expense to pray for the sick in the name of Jesus Christ. While bringing a revival to this nation (America) and sharing the gospel of Jesus in India and throughout the seven continents, David has built a ministry rooted in loving Jesus and loving people through sharing the gospel of Jesus and demonstrating the living word through healing, miracles, deliverance, signs, and wonders.

For more information, go to dtim.org

David Turner International Ministries

EXPERIENCE JESUS

Experience Jesus is a FREE mobile app that delivers discipleship tools directly to your phone. The app has over 350 biblical teaching shows available for streaming, bible memorization tools, daily rhemas and 5-minute prayers.

Download FREE today on all Apple and Andriod devices. Go to experience-jesus.com for more.

Continue your reading with

SEEDS OF FAITH

By David Turner

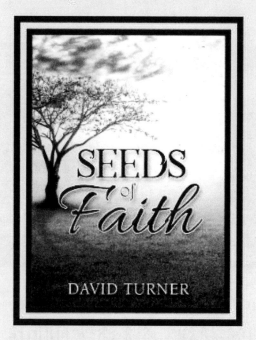

SEEDS OF FAITH takes the reader on a journey through the landscape of the miraculous. David Turner uses his personal experiences with Jesus Christ to chronicle a life marked by an amazing supernatural relationship with a living God. Seeds of Faith will bring the Grace, Love and Joy of a living God into the forefront of your daily life. It will change your thoughts and heart about miracles and reveal the unimaginable kindness that God has for people

Available for purchase on Amazon,com or FREE download on dtim.org